THE TEMPEST

Text and Performance

DAVID L. HIRST

M

MACMILLAN

First published 1984

Published by
Higher and Further Education Division
MACMILLAN PUBLISHERS LTD
Houndmills, Basingstoke, Hampshire RG21 2XS
and London
Companies and representatives
throughout the world

Typeset by
Wessex Typesetters Ltd
Frome, Somerset

Printed in Hong Kong

British Library Cataloguing in Publication Data
Hirst, David L.
The tempest.—(Text and performance)
1. Shakespeare, William. Tempest
I. Title   II. Series
822.3′3   PR2833
ISBN 0-333-34465-0

CONTENTS

Illustrations will be found in Part Two

ACKNOWLEDGEMENTS

Quotations of the text of the play and references to it are from the New Penguin Shakespeare edition (1968), edited by Anne Righter.

Source details for the illustrations are given with the relevant captions to the photographs.

I should like to thank Derek Jarman and Dr Jonathan Miller for giving up so much of their time in discussing their productions with me. I have received valuable assistance from Caroline Wilson at the National Theatre and Laura Lombardi at the Piccolo Teatro di Milano who so kindly put a wealth of documentary material at my disposal. I am also indebted to Dottoressa Annamaria Cascetta for her advice and help, and to RAI television in Milan for enabling me to study its film of the Strehler production. I am grateful to Antony J. Simlick for typing the final version.

GENERAL EDITOR'S PREFACE

For many years a mutual suspicion existed between the theatre director and the literary critic of drama. Although in the first half of the century there were important exceptions, such was the rule. A radical change of attitude, however, has taken place over the last thirty years. Critics and directors now increasingly recognise the significance of each other's work and acknowledge their growing awareness of interdependence. Both interpret the same text, but do so according to their different situations and functions. Without the director, the designer and the actor, a play's existence is only partial. They revitalise the text with action, enabling the drama to live fully at each performance. The academic critic investigates the script to elucidate its textual problems, understand its conventions and discover how it operates. He may also propose his view of the work, expounding what he considers to be its significance.

Dramatic texts belong therefore to theatre and to literature. The aim of the 'Text and Performance' series is to achieve a fuller recognition of how both enhance our enjoyment of the play. Each volume follows the same basic pattern. Part One provides a critical introduction to the play under discussion, using the techniques and criteria of the literary critic in examining the manner in which the work operates through language, imagery and action. Part Two takes the enquiry further into the play's theatricality by focusing on selected productions of recent times so as to illustrate points of contrast and comparison in the interpretation of different directors and actors, and to demonstrate how the drama has worked on the modern stage. In this way the series seeks to provide a lively and informative introduction to major plays in their text and performance.

MICHAEL SCOTT

PLOT SYNOPSIS AND SOURCES

The banished Duke of Milan, Prospero, conjures up a storm to shipwreck old enemies on his island of exile. Twelve years previously his brother Antonio had conspired with Alonzo, King of Naples, to seize the dukedom. Prospero's sole friend at court, Gonzalo, had provided supplies for his enforced flight and his valuable collection of occult books.

Ariel, his spirit-servant, assures him the ship is intact, its crew and passengers safe, with Ferdinand (Alonzo's son and heir) separated from the others. The young prince is brought to Miranda, Prospero's daughter, and they fall in love. Prospero must act quickly before his magical power declines. He enforces hard labour on Ferdinand to test him, and spell-binds the court party into deep slumber through Ariel's magical music. But Antonio and Alonzo's brother, Sebastian, do not succumb, and they plot to murder the sleeping king. Ariel foils their plan at the last moment.

Meanwhile two other survivors, Trinculo, a jester, and Stephano, a drunken butler, fall in with Prospero's credulous native slave Caliban, who offers to exchange masters if Stephano will kill Prospero.

Prospero presents the guilty courtiers with a banquet which disappears to present Ariel as a vengeful harpy. Alonzo, believing that his own crime against the exiled duke has been punished through the death of Ferdinand, is deeply affected. Prospero rewards the constancy of the lovers with a celebratory betrothal masque.

At its climax, suddenly recalling Caliban's conspiracy, he transforms the spirit-actors into dogs who hound the miscreants. The sense of danger narrowly averted, and Ariel's suggestion that his further harshness in paralysing the court party is excessive, prompt Prospero to renounce his magic. He brings everyone together, thanks Gonzalo for his fidelity, and confronts his enemies. Ferdinand is reunited with his grateful father, who breaks the pact with Antonio and obliges him to restore the dukedom to Prospero. Caliban regrets his misplaced confidence in Stephano. As the royal and ducal groups prepare for Italy, Ariel is given his freedom, and Caliban regains the island.

SOURCES

The play has no direct narrative source. Three different influences (discussed in detail in section 2 of Part One, below) have left their mark on it: contemporary accounts of voyages to the Bermudas; Medea's incantation from Ovid's *Metamorphoses* (book VII); and Montaigne's essay, *Of Cannibals*.

PART ONE: TEXT

1 INTRODUCTION

The Tempest is a play about power. The protagonist is a Renaissance ruler who through assiduous study has gained a knowledge and control of the world which have the force of magic. In this drama Shakespeare contrasts the urge to seize political power with the desire to impose a higher level of ethical and spiritual values through the exercise of the will. The play is the ultimate variation on one of the dramatist's favourite themes: the contrast between the pragmatic political realist and the philosophical idealist.

Such a confrontation is basic to the two cycles of English history plays in which Henry VI, the saintly recluse, is brought into conflict with Richard III, the unscrupulous opportunist and the artist, Richard II, is deposed by the man of action, Bolingbroke. Prospero, too, has been deposed, but he has a more practical strength in his application of learning by means of magic.

From the extension of reason Prospero derives a power which he uses in an attempt to influence everyone on the island. The self-control he has so studiously acquired is imparted to Ferdinand, who learns how to love more deeply. Unlike Trinculo and Stephano, who become slaves to passion in the company of Caliban, Ferdinand masters his emotions and proves himself a worthy heir to Naples.

Furthermore, since Prospero exercises a force over everyone, manipulating the characters while employing music and spectacle to divert them, he represents the artist, Shakespeare himself, who is posing a fundamental question in this play: What is the power of the dramatist to influence and change the world?

2 SHAKESPEARE'S 'FINAL' PLAY

It is as though Shakespeare, through his magician-prince, were evaluating the different types of power proper to the magus, the ruler and the artist. This concern gives the play a sense of finality: an impression that Shakespeare is summing up everything he had written before, and reaching a balanced conclusion. We know that he went on to write at least a part of *Henry VIII* but this does not impair the valedictory tone of *The Tempest*. It is dangerously restrictive, however, to view the play as essentially concerned with autobiography. Wilson Knight has most persuasively argued a case for seeing a reflection of every previous Shakespearean drama in *The Tempest*, but it is important not to underestimate the social and political aims of the playwright. In Prospero's renunciation of his magic there is clearly a reference to Shakespeare's intended retirement, but the play is concerned with other issues than the personal and the artistic. Prospero, like Marlowe's Faustus, is a Renaissance thinker, trying to better himself and the world. He seeks new realms of knowledge and is representative of the newly-discovered potential of mankind. *The Tempest* is also Shakespeare's last political drama. Through the repetition of the original usurpation both in the attempted assassination of Alonzo and the plot of Caliban against Prospero, we are confronted with the relentless machinations of contemporary statecraft.

The Sources

We can observe Shakespeare's aims and intentions most clearly by a consideration of his sources. He was receptive to several influences which leave their mark on the play, but it is significant that no history, chronicle, drama or *novella* guided him either in the construction of the work or the development of the plot. The originality of *The Tempest* is one of its most striking features. However, it is particularly revealing to discover in the play debts to three sources which Shakespeare utilised in a very precise and direct way. The firm impression left by the source material is the clearest pointer to the dramatist's central concerns.

(a) Contemporary Voyages. In May 1609 a fleet of nine ships with five hundred colonists sailed from Plymouth to strengthen John Smith's colony in Virginia. On 25 July the flagship *Sea Adventure* (carrying the admiral, Sir John Somers, and the new governor of the colony, Sir Thomas Gates) was separated from the rest of the fleet in a storm off the Bermudas. News of the mishap reached England before the end of the year and the ship was presumed to have been lost. But the whole crew had in fact managed to reach land and repair their ship, and in May 1610 they arrived safely in Virginia. When this news reached London in September of that year their preservation was regarded as a miracle and many narratives of their experience were published. Relevant to *The Tempest* are Silvester Jourdain's *Discovery of the Barmudas*, the Council of Virginia's *True Declaration of the State of the Colonie in Virginia*, and a letter by William Strachey known as *A True Reportory of the Wracke*. The first two were published in 1610, the third not until 1625. Since it is Strachey's report which contains the closest verbal correspondences with *The Tempest*, we have ample proof of Shakespeare's friendship with members of the Virginia company as well as of his interest in their project, since he must have read the letter in manuscript.

These narratives fired Shakespeare's imagination. The accounts both of a new world and of explorers apparently preserved by magic confirmed the hopes and aspirations of the man of the Renaissance. Jourdain speaks of the paradisal quality of the island concluding: 'whereas it hath beene, and is still accounted, the most dangerous, infortunate, and most forlorne place in the world, it is in truth the richest, healthfullest and pleasing land . . . as ever a man set foot upon' (*Discovery of the Barmudas*, pp. 7–10). Strachey's description of St Elmo's fire and of the fresh water supplies on the island find close echoes in Ariel's speech [I ii 196–201] and Caliban's account [II ii 151] respectively. But it is the deeper philosophical and ethical implications of this experience which were to inspire the most fundamental paradoxes of Shakespeare's drama. *The True Declaration* asks: 'What is there in all this tragicall comoedie that should discourage us with impossibilitie of the enterprise?

when of all the Fleete, one only Ship, by a secret leake was indangered, and yet in the gulfe of Despair was so graciously preserved. *Quae videtur poena est medicina*: that which we accompt a punishment of evill is but a medicine against evill' (from *Tracts and Other Papers*, ed. P. Force, vol. 3, p. 11). And it is William Strachey's letter which, commenting on the impossibility of reforming the savage Indian (an incident narrated after the arrival in Virginia), underlines the central theme of *The Tempest*: colonisation. 'It did not a little trouble the Lieutenant Governor, who since his first landing in the Countrey, how justly provoked, would not by any means be wrought to a violent proceeding against them [the natives] for all the practice of villany, with which they daily indangered our men, thinking it possible by a more tractable course to winne them to a better condition: but now being startled by this, he well perceived how little a fair and noble entreatie works upon a barbarous disposition, and therefore in some measure purposed to be revenged' (*Purchas His Pilgrimes*, vol. 4, p. 1755). From the germ of this incident was to develop the complex and ironic relationship between Prospero and Caliban which is fundamental to the play.

(b) Montaigne. Another work concerning voyages to the New World is known to have influenced Shakespeare even more directly. This is Montaigne's *Of Cannibals* which is one of the *Essais* (1580–88) translated by John Florio and published in 1603. Montaigne tells us: 'I have had long time dwelling with me a man who for the space of ten or twelve yeares had dwelt in that other world, which in our age was lately discovered in those parts where Villegaigon first landed and surnamed Antartike France. This discoverie, of so infinit and vast a countrie, seemeth worthy great consideration.' His 'consideration' centres on a contrast between the civilised world and the natural life of the savage. For Montaigne, the cannibals 'seem therefore so barbarous unto me because they have received very little fashion from humane wit and are yet neere their originall naturalitie. The lawes of nature doe yet command them which are but little bastardised by ours.' He idealised the cannibals who more resemble Swift's Houyhnhnms than 'savage and deformed slave(s)'; but Caliban has a very real nobility and Shakespeare makes us aware of the ambiguous

overtones of usurpation in Prospero's colonisation. The eulogy central to Montaigne's essay is incorporated very directly into the play where it forms the basis of Gonzalo's description of the ideal commonwealth [II ii 141–62]: 'It is a nation . . . that hath no kind of traffike, no knowledge of Letters, no intelligence of numbers, no name of magistrate, nor of politike superioritie; no use of service, of riches or of povertie; no contracts, no successions, no partitions, no occupation but idle; no respect of kindred but common, no apparell but naturall, no manuring of the lands, no use of wine, corne or mettle' (Montaigne, *Essay* xxx). Gonzalo's speech is the play's touchstone. The vision of utopia is ambiguous: the 'honest old councellor' is easily ridiculed by the practical men, Antonio and Sebastian, and yet they are in turn revealed as cynical and untrustworthy.

(c) Ovid. The third example of Shakespeare's employment of existing source material is the adaptation of Medea's incantation in Ovid's *Metamorphoses* [VII, 197–209] which forms the basis of Prospero's farewell to his art. It may strike the modern reader as unusual that, at the climactic point of the play, the dramatist should rely so heavily on another work. Moreover, close examination of the passage reveals that Shakespeare was familiar not only with Golding's celebrated translation (published in 1567) but with the original. To the Renaissance mind it did not appear derivative but creative to draw on familiar material and reshape it to fresh ends. Prospero's renunciation of his magical power is the turning-point of the play, and Shakespeare seeks to enrich this moment through allusion. We are made to feel at this point in the drama more accutely than elsewhere the significance of the classical background which profoundly informs *The Tempest*, both in its echoes of Virgil's *Aeneid* and in the precise structuring of its five acts along the lines of the theories of neo-classical tragi-comedy. At the play's climax the old world confronts the new and Shakespeare scrutinises the values of both through an analysis of the potential of magic.

Romance

Though *The Tempest* has a formal precision which sets it apart

from the works which immediately preceded it – *Pericles*,
Cymbeline and *The Winter's Tale* – it shares with them images and
themes which bind the last plays together as a group. These
dramas are all romances. Their material is remote and
improbable; there are many supernatural elements; and, while
being in a predominantly tragic vein, they all have a happy
ending. In terms of plot they all have strong echoes of
Shakespeare's most seminal tragedy, *King Lear*. The central
character in each play is a ruler who through misunderstanding
either perpetrates or sustains the effects of an evil deed which
results in the loss of loved ones: in each case a child, and in two
instances a wife. Suffering follows, in the midst of which seeds of
a new life are germinating. Finally there is a restoration of loved
ones, and a fairer prosperity issues. *Lear* does not end at this
point: the tragic harvest is to be reaped, but it follows this plot
outline up to Lear's awakening in the English camp. The
romances are in fact closer to the play Shakespeare used as
source: the anonymous *Chronicle History of King Leir*. It is as
though Shakespeare felt compelled to return to this play,
reshaping it until it took perfect form in *The Tempest*.

These plays have more in common than similarity of the plot,
however. In the course of the events dramatised, two recurring
images of symbolic significance are to be observed. They are
the presence of storm, and the undertaking of a pilgrimage.

Lear betakes himself to the heath in a storm; Thaisa
supposedly dies in childbirth during a storm at sea; Perdita is
abandoned as a baby while a storm is brewing; and *The Tempest*
both opens with a storm at sea and also narrates the exposure of
Prospero and Miranda to the elements when exiled from
Milan. The idea of a character struggling towards self-
knowledge and happiness through hardship and exile is
contained in the pilgrimages which determine the plot of these
plays. It is a harsh journey for both Lear and Gloucester from
the royal palace to Dover, but the one finds 'reason in
madness', the other insight in blindness. A pilgrimage is the
dominating motif in *Pericles*; it recurs in *Cymbeline* in Imogen's
departure for Milford Haven, and reappears in Perdita's
journey from Sicily to Bohemia and back again. Prospero's 'sea
sorrows' bring him to the island where he perfects his
knowledge, whilst Alonzo's wanderings in search of Ferdinand

effect in him contrition through spiritual purgation. The over-riding idea in these late plays is of breakdown followed by reconstruction. Family bonds are abused, relatives are separated, and we are presented with a potentially tragic world of suffering and loss. Even in the tragedies, however, Shakespeare shows us elements of good which are not destroyed by the tragic pattern – Horatio, Edgar, Malcolm – and at the end of these plays we glimpse a new generation in which there is renewed hope. In the romances Shakespeare focuses on this seed of new life, watches it germinate and presents its final triumph over evil. Love and forgiveness replace hatred and cruelty; the characters are re-born. In *The Tempest* old friends, old enemies, long-lost and newly-lost relatives all unite, but with a renewed truth and honesty on Shakespeare's part. Gone is the fairy-tale ending of *Pericles*, the clumsy absurd reunion of *Cymbeline*, the miracle which terminates *The Winter's Tale*. Miranda has found a 'brave new world', one which contains not only her repentant father-in-law but also the unchanged Antonio and Sebastian as well as the worthless Trinculo and Stephano.

It is difficult to feel any sympathy for critics, such as Rose Abdelnour Zimbado, who insist that *The Tempest* has nothing in common with the other romances. The strong note of realism on which the play ends should rather make us aware of the complexity of the dénouement. Lytton Strachey was the first writer to object to the attitude of romantic critics, such as Dowden, who saw the play as Shakespeare's presentation of his own final attainment of peaceful serenity in forgiveness, wisdom and peace. For Strachey this play represents Shakespeare not 'on the heights' but 'in the depths'. He draws attention to the intensity of the bitterness in the dramatisation of evil, and sees Prospero as 'self-opinionated' and 'sour'. His conclusion is that Shakespeare was disillusioned, having grown 'bored with people, bored with real life, bored with drama'.

Until the comparatively recent studies of the Polish critic Jan Kott, Lytton Strachey's approach has found little support. Kott goes further, seeing *The Tempest* as the most bitter of Shakespeare's plays. He draws attention to Gonzalo's evocation of an innocent community which gives way to attempted murder, and to the vision of the Golden Age in Act IV which turns into a savage man-hunt. For him the play represents the lost hope of the Renaissance and the author's conviction that theatre is unable to change the world.

Kott's critique stands in sharp contrast to the studies of Arthur Quiller-Couch, E. K. Chambers and G. B. Harrison, which are closer to Dowden in stressing the positive elements of the play. Kott, however, as we shall see, has had a far more radical influence on directors than any other critic, not only because his emphasis is more theatrical, but because he has underlined the fact that the powerful dramatic potential of the play is only released by a thorough exploration of its contradictions and ambiguity.

3   NATURE AND NURTURE

Ethical Issues

The central theme of the final plays is the conflict of nature and art. It is a conflict which in Shakespeare's analysis is productive of the most significant and meaningful insights into life. From the rejection of the unnatural and the artificial in *Pericles*, through the contrast of country and court in *Cymbeline* and *The Winter's Tale*, to the confrontation of nature and nurture in *The Tempest*, Shakespeare expands the topic which has been the subject of exhaustive analysis in *King Lear*. The development in the romances, however, is towards a more objective philosophical analysis of the ethical issues involved. The long discussion between Polixenes and Perdita in the sheep-shearing scene of *The Winter's Tale* concludes with the paradox that 'art is nature' since 'nature is made better by no mean / But nature makes that mean' [iv iv 89–90]: an argument which is to be extended further in *The Tempest*.

The most powerful dramatic expression of this theme is Prospero's rage at the frustration of his plans through the conspiracy of the clowns. He calls Caliban 'A devil, a born devil, on whose nature / Nature can never stick' – the versification underlines the violent juxtaposition of two worlds. Prospero is the representative of the world of nurture, of civilisation, of art. His ethic is that of cultivating and improving the raw nature of which Caliban is the prime exemplar. The fullest expression of the teacher's disappointment – the governor's feeling that he has been betrayed – is conveyed in his regret that his 'pains' though 'humanely taken' have been 'lost, quite lost'. Judged from the point of view of a superior culture, Caliban is the ungrateful, graceless savage who is incapable of appreciating the higher values of a nobler race.

But the situation is not so simple. Caliban stands firmly at the centre of the play, the pointer to the different criteria of two worlds. He represents, as we shall see, the noble savage as well as the brute; and it is his unspoilt nature which throws into relief the viciousness of the civilisation which both trains the political unscrupulousness of Antonio and corrupts the morals of Trinculo and Stephano. Moreover, Prospero's anger at Caliban here is personally motivated, not only because his show for Ferdinand and Miranda has been spoilt, but because he had 'forgot the foul conspiracy'. His fury expresses itself in his determination to 'plague them all, even to roaring', and accordingly he orders the spirits who have just presented the nuptial masque to transform themselves into dogs and hound the offenders. The kindly overseer has become the savage tyrant who has resorted to the barbarities attributed to the contemporary Spaniards in their hunting of native slaves.

Nowhere in the play do we see Prospero in such an unattractive light, and this should alert us to the complexity of the ethical issues. The ambiguity resides essentially in the two approaches to the term 'nature'. At the time Shakespeare was writing the play, two contrasting views were held: nature is that which man spoils; and, alternatively, nature is that which, because it is defective, needs cultivation. In *Henry V*, at the end of his long speech on the state of France which as a result of the war with England has been allowed to run wild, the Duke of Burgundy – lamenting that 'nothing teems / But hateful docks, rough thistles, kecksies, burs' – terms this state of nature unaided by art 'unnatural'. It is a paradox which haunts Shakespeare's drama and reaches its sharpest point of focus in his final play. Another aspect of the unnatural is seen in Prospero's moral condemnation of Antonio: 'I do forgive thee', he says, 'unnatural though thou art.' The implication of his criticism can be seen more clearly two lines earlier in the explanation that Antonio has 'expelled remorse and nature'. These are precisely the two essentially human qualities – pity and natural bonds of affection – which are so ruthlessly suppressed by Lady Macbeth when she says:

> . . .   make thick my blood
> Stop up the access and passage to *remorse*
> That no compunctious visitings of *nature*
> Shake my fell purpose. . . .   [*Macbeth*, I v 43–6]

Civilisation should provide an education which controls and utilises to the full the natural potential of humanity. It should not be a means for suppressing and destroying natural instincts. Prospero's condemnation of his brother could apply to himself, both in his treatment of Caliban, the natural man, and in his exclusion of human feeling in the concentration – through his art – on his own project.

Colonisation

The dramatic strength of *The Tempest* resides in the recurrent and violent shifts of perspective which force us constantly to reassess the situation. When Caliban states:

> This island's mine, by Sycorax my mother,
> Which thou tak'st from me. . . .

and adds:

> For I am all the subjects that you have,
> Which first was mine own King; . . .   [I ii 331–2, 341–2]

we see Prospero as the usurper on the island. Shakespeare emphasises the point by having Caliban describe Prospero's treatment of him in terms that recall the attitude of the patronising coloniser exploiting the natural resources of his new-found conquest:

> . . .   When thou cam'st first
> Thou strok'st me, and made much of me; would'st give me
> Water with berries in't, and teach me how
> To name the bigger light, and how the less,

That burn by day and night. And then I loved thee,
And showed thee all the qualities o' th' isle,
The fresh springs, brine-pits, barren place and fertile.

[I ii 332-8]

Prospero's attitude to Caliban when he first arrives on the island is benevolent; he seeks to impart his own culture to the savage native. But his attempt is not merely futile: it gives Caliban a new weapon, language, and Caliban's curses are the most powerful condemnation of Prospero's way of life. We are made to reflect on the difference between the education Caliban has received and that which Miranda enjoys, and to consider whether Caliban's natural method of expression was necessarily inferior to the language of his oppressor.

There is, certainly, a danger of interpreting the presentation of Caliban too much through a contemporary perspective, and criticising Prospero in terms of more enlightened racial theories. But to see the native islander as nothing more than a 'savage and deformed slave' is to fail to come to terms with the central dynamic of the play. Prospero's savage description later – when he tells us 'even as his body uglier grows / So his mind cankers' – is not an objective one: this tells us more about the master than the slave. Caliban's ugliness is in the eye of the beholder. It is only after his attempted rape that Miranda sees him as 'a villain . . . I do not love to look on' and that Prospero's attitude changes. To Trinculo and Stephano he is not a thing of terror, but a 'mooncalf', alternately 'a most ridiculous monster', a 'poor monster' and a 'brave monster'. He is, of course, very dangerous: his attempted rape of Miranda and assassination of Prospero reveal his basic urges towards lust and violence. These are the fundamental aspects of raw nature and are part of humanity. Inflamed with drink, Stephano 'begins to have bloody thoughts' and looks forward to ravishing Miranda. At the end of the play Prospero has to confess: 'this thing of darkness I / Acknowledge mine.'

The theme of colonisation is most sharply focussed in Gonzalo's discussion of his ideal commonwealth [II i]. This takes up the topic of nature versus art, and parallels the examination of the relationship between coloniser and native in Prospero's handling of Caliban. Again the issue is by no means

simple. Gonzalo idealises the natural life, but criticism is
provided not only by Antonio and Sebastian but by the
self-contradictory aspects of Gonzalo's argument. His initial
proposal, 'Had I plantation of this isle, my lord', is interrupted
by Antonio who twists Gonzalo's meaning of 'colonisation' to
that of 'planting', and comments sarcastically: 'He'd sow it
with nettle seed.' It is a clever dramatic stroke to place this vital
argument in the mouth of an old, garrulous courtier who is,
moreover, 'ministering occasion' in an attempt to distract
Alonzo from his grief at the loss of Ferdinand. But it should not
lead us to believe either that the topic is irrelevant or so easily to
be ridiculed as Antonio and Sebastian suppose.

  Gonzalo is proposing his own version of a 'brave new world',
such as Montaigne envisaged and the travellers to Virginia
hoped to rediscover. Gonzalo's reference to the 'Golden Age' is
an allusion to the mythological age of plenty and innocence
ruled by Saturn, when the earth provided for all man's
requirements and he needed to do no work. Virgil in his Fourth
Eclogue celebrates The Age of Gold and envisages the return to
earth of Astraea (Justice) who has left the world as a
consequence of man's folly and sin. The impossibility of finding
or establishing such a perfect society is the underlying theme of
the whole drama, but Shakespeare is concerned to show both
the ideal and real. Hence, Gonzalo's vision of a world where
'nature should bring forth / Of it own kind, all foison, all
abundance / To feed my innocent people', is qualified by the
fact that – as Antonio is quick to point out – 'the latter end of his
commonwealth forgets the beginning'. Gonzalo would be king
and yet have 'no sovereignty'. This is the basic problem. To
establish a workable and just society, law and order are
necessary. Such a utopia as Gonzalo envisages, where all men
are equal, denies the principle of degree revered by
Elizabethans and Jacobeans alike. As Samuel Purchas, the
author of the two most important collections of Jacobean travel
literature and a supporter of the coloniser in his usurpation of
the rights of the ignorant native, puts it:

  Can a Leopard change its spots? Can a Savage remayning a Savage
  be civill? Were not wee our selves made and not borne civill in our
  Progenitors days? and were not Ceasar's Britaines as brutish as

Virginians? The Romane swords were best teachers of civilitie to this & other Countries neare us.

(Purchas His Pilgrimes, vol. 4, p. 1755)

The contradiction basic to Gonzalo's description points to the dominant conflict in the play between master and servant. This is presented in a powerful fundamental way in the contrast between Prospero's handling of Ariel and Caliban in their first scene. Caliban is the unwilling slave, Ariel the more pliant servant. These terms echo throughout the rest of the play with an insistence which is ultimately musical. Shakespeare rings every possible variation on this theme, discerned at first in the context of the coloniser and the native but working through the contrasted scenes of the drama so as to be given comic and tragic tones as well as linking the world of harsh political reality with that of emotional and philosophical idealism.

Ferdinand is forced to undergo harsh slavery in his log-bearing so that he may conquer the Caliban in himself. The finer selfless qualities of both lovers are expressed through the interdependence of master and servant. Miranda says, 'I'll be your servant/Whether you will or no'; to which Ferdinand replies, 'My mistress dearest/And I thus humble ever'. In persuading Sebastian to follow his example and seize political power, Antonio seeks to repeat the act of usurpation which is the starting-point of the story and which receives burlesque treatment in the plot of Trinculo and Stephano against Prospero. Caliban is only too ready to change one master for another; but as the monarch he worships becomes more and more a slave to drink, he realises the futility of his assassination attempt and the folly of his treachery.

A related theme of the play, one which gradually develops a note of relentless obsession, is that of exploitation. When Trinculo first sees Caliban his thought is to take him to England and display him in a fair. 'When they will not give a doit to relieve a lame beggar', he comments, 'they will lay out ten to see a dead Indian' [ii i 32–4]. When Sebastian catches sight of him at the end of the play with his bedraggled companions and asks, 'What things are these, my Lord Antonio? Will money buy 'em?', he receives the reply: 'one of them is a plain fish and no doubt marketable' [v i 264–6].

Ultimately all these comments point relentlessly to Prospero. We are forced to see his conduct in the same light. Of Caliban he admits: 'We cannot miss him: he does make our fire / Fetch in our wood and serves in offices / That profit us.' It is the confession of an exploiter.

4 Magic

Sorcery versus Natural Philosophy

Prospero is not only a coloniser, however. He is also a magician. It is when we consider Caliban and Ariel in the context of the supernatural that the savage and the spirit assume a quite different significance. Shakespeare uses Caliban as a pointer to the evil black magic which is the antithesis of the beneficent white magic Prospero employs. However sympathetic we may feel to the exploited native, Shakespeare does not allow us to experience anything but repugnance and fear in considering his birth and the function of his mother's sorcery. Sycorax – a figure all the more disturbing because we do not see her – personifies all the terrors and horrors which the Elizabethans and Jacobeans channelled into their savage hunting of witches. She enables us by contrast to see Prospero as a quite different exploiter of the supernatural, as a man of wisdom seeking to employ his knowledge for the betterment of the world around him.

Shakespeare was writing at a time when magic was taken very seriously. Many of the leading minds of his age were attempting through an expansion of scientific study and research to contact forces beyond the mundane, the natural. These men were in turn feared by the forces of the Counter-Reformation and other upholders of traditional interests. Giordano Bruno, Italy's leading occult philosopher, was burnt at the stake in 1600; Dr John Dee, England's most important student of the supernatural, died in poverty and disgrace in 1608. Both these men were examples of a vital Renaissance phenomenon: the neoplatonic mage. Neo-platonism (as expounded most forcefully in the works of Marcilio Ficino and Giovanni Pico della Mirandola at the Medici court in Florence in the late fifteenth century) was a studious attempt to christianise the teachings of the great Greek philosopher. Plato – notably in the *Symposium* – had argued that man must ascend by degrees from a contemplation of physical beauty to an appreciation of spiritual truth: a thesis which had cost his philosophic master, Socrates, his life. In the early Italian Renaissance this doctrine was logically extended to embrace Christian belief and – under Pico most notably – assumed occult significance through the employment of the magical properties of the Jewish Cabala. It was Henricus Cornelius Agrippa (1486–1535) who was to pursue the research much further and formulate a precise technique for the exploration of supernatural forces.

Agrippa published in 1533 his influential work *De Occulta Philosophia* which summarised the work of Italian scholars and ventured into areas of which they had been more wary. Of its three books, the first is about natural magic, or magic in the elemental world, teaching how to arrange substances in an occult manner so as to effect magical operations. The second book is about celestial magic, or how to attract and influence the stars. Its operations are based on mathematical science. The third book is concerned with ceremonial magic, directed towards the supercelestial world of angelic spirits. Agrippa sees the magus as *divinorum cultor e interpres*, 'a studious observer and expounder of divine things' – his art being 'the absolute perfection of natural philosophy', an amalgam of astrology, alchemy and ceremonial magic.

The work of Agrippa had a profound influence on the English magician Dr John Dee (1527–1608), whose vast library contained all the major studies of science, philosophy and the occult: three areas of research which in the late sixteenth century overlapped, complementing one another rather than falling into what a later, more rationalist, age distinguishes as science and pseudo-science. Like Prospero, Dee had a library which was 'dukedom enough'. He, too, was to lose it: it was burnt by assiduous witch-hunters. Through his geographical knowledge and mathematical expertise, Dee was of immense assistance to the early navigators. Indeed, he conceived of his skills as being essentially in the service of promoting the Elizabethan empire, in colonising and improving the world. But his work was utterly inimical to the more sceptical, and conservative, James I who came to the throne in 1603. Dee was obliged to defend himself, and he did so in a famous letter to the Archbishop of Canterbury (printed in 1604, but written earlier) which both echoes the neo-platonism of Agrippa and also defines the nature and the aim of the magic employed by Shakespeare's exponent of this art, Prospero. Dee tells us that from his youth it had pleased the Almighty

> to insinuate into my hart, an insatiable zeale, and desire to knowe his truth: And in him, and by him, incessantly to seeke, and listen after the same; by the true philosophical method and harmony: proceeding and ascending ... *gradatim* from things visible, to consider of things invisible; from things bodily, to conceive of things spiritual; from things transitorie, and momentarie, to meditate of things permanent; by things mortall ... to have some perceiuerance of immortality. ...
> (John Dee, *A Letter Containing a ... Discourse Apologeticall*; in J. Crossley (ed.), *Autobiographical Tracts* [Manchester, 1851] p. 72)

Like Agrippa and Dee, Prospero employs a type of magic which is firmly grounded in scientific reality. By a gradual, lengthy process he has learned how to exploit natural phenomena. His arrival on the island gives him the opportunity to release a more subtle energy in the form of Ariel. Dee believed that he had achieved with his associate, Edward Kelley, the power of conjuring angels. Prospero, in harnessing the force represented by Ariel to his own ends, considerably extends the range of his influence.

Sycorax could not attain this level of magic. (Ariel is 'A spirit too delicate to act her earthy and abhored commands'.) She can only enchain the power she cannot employ. Her sphere of operation is much more mundane. We learn of her 'mischiefs manifold, and sorceries terrible / To enter human hearing'. Hers is a negative, destructive magic. Significantly, she seems to have passed on none of her powers to Caliban.

Prospero, by contrast, works almost exclusively through Ariel: the 'airy spirit' is literally his medium. It is through his own scientific – specifically astrological – knowledge that he is aware of the unique opportunity offered him by the approach of his enemies. This comes about through his 'prescience'. Thereafter he works through Ariel, conjuring up the storm in which his spirit 'flames amazement'; splitting the shipwrecked crew 'in troops about the island'; drawing Ferdinand to the cell (through Ariel in the form of a Nymph of the sea); lulling the court to sleep; conjuring the magical banquet (with Ariel subsequently as a Harpy); and presenting the betrothal masque through 'some vanity of [his] art'. It is this spirit who will be responsible subsequently for his change of heart which leads to the renunciation of his magic and thus to Ariel's freedom: a complex development which marks the turning point in the play.

> So rare a wondered father and a wise
> Makes this place Paradise.   [IV i 123–4]

remarks Ferdinand during the presentation of the betrothal masque. Prospero is attempting through his magic to redeem fallen nature. He seeks to transcend worldly values and create a utopia, an ideal society. The innocence and chastity of the young lovers is vital to this. His insistence that Ferdinand does not 'Break her virgin knot before / All sanctimonious cere-monies may / With full and holy rite be minister'd' is not the over-zealous concern of a prurient father, but the profound awareness of the magus of the necessity and consequent power of chastity. It is as important as the silence he enjoins when warning 'No tongue, all eyes, be silent'.

But the neo-platonic idealism of Prospero is a far cry from the drunken indulgence of Caliban and his companions which will shortly wreck the seer's well-laid plans. Shakespeare is honest enough to show us that the operation of magic is specifically circumscribed, not only by the limitations of Prospero's sphere of influence, but also by the intransigent nature of his raw material.

Prospero's 'Project'

What precisely is Prospero trying to achieve, then, through his employment of magic? This question is fundamental to the play; it should be the first consideration of critic and director alike. At the beginning of Act v Prospero tells us:

> Now does my project gather to a head:
> My charms crack not, my spirits obey and time
> Goes upright with his carriage. . . .

This is not the first time we have heard of this 'project'. When Ariel awakens the sleeping courtiers and prevents the assassination attempt of Antonio and Sebastian, he says:

> My master through his art forsees the danger
> That you, his friend, are in, and sends me forth –
> For else his project dies – to keep them living! [ii i 302–4]

Evidently Prospero has a very clear idea of what exactly he is trying to achieve. If we consider the careful sequence of actions from the start of the play we can observe what this plan is.

Aware that 'bountiful fortune' has provided him 'by accident most strange' with a unique opportunity to interfere in the destiny of his own country and family, he determines to do everything in his power to reverse the events which occurred twelve years previously. First of all he puts the fear of God into everyone on the ship; and then, having ensured everyone comes ashore with 'not a hair perished', he separates the survivors of the shipwreck into different groups. This serves several functions. It allows him to operate on the protagonists separately and in turn; it also ensures that the profound emotional shock of (supposedly) losing loved ones will have a therapeutic effect on the victims. Both Ferdinand and Alonzo, through exposure to an intense suffering, are likely to be more psychologically and spiritually open to the fresh experiences they will encounter on the island. Prospero's next step is to lead Ferdinand to Miranda. The magician has done everything he can to bring them together and to prepare them – she through her father's teaching, he through the loss of his father – for this crucial meeting. What Prospero cannot do is make them fall in love. That stands as surely outside the sphere of his influence as does the ship until it providentially approaches the island. But they do fall in love, Miranda for the first time, Ferdinand in a far deeper way than he has experienced before. Prospero breathes a sigh of relief. His aside, 'It works!', is charged with significance. The work of the neo-platonic teacher, the improver of minds and spirits does not end there, however. He puts their love to the test, forcing them to learn more deeply the nature of their mutual interdependence.

This is extended through a sequence of three scenes: the meeting [I ii], the testing [III i] and the reward [IV]. In order to supervise this, Prospero is obliged to put the other elements of his project temporarily out of action. Though omniscient he is not omnipotent. He is firmly circumscribed by astrological forces converging to his advantage at this moment:

> . . .   my zenith doth depend upon
> A most auspicious star, whose influence
> If now I court not, but omit, my fortunes
> Will ever after droop. . . .   [I ii 181–4]

He must act quickly; in short, he has barely three hours. He thus lulls the court to sleep, intending to return to them when his plans for Miranda and Ferdinand are well underway. Having observed the testing of the lovers, he can thus turn to the court and confront the 'three men of sin' with their guilt. The situation in some ways is comparable with that on the road to Damascus, where God confronts St Paul, provoking a spiritual crisis which has been interpreted – notably in Strindberg's play *To Damascus* – as the equivalent of a psychological breakdown, necessary for the undertaking of a fresh, more fulfilled life. He can then confront his old enemies in person, demand the restitution of his dukedom and establish a 'brave new world' through the union of Milan and Naples in the marriage of Ferdinand and Miranda.

His project begins and ends with Miranda. For twelve years he has lived alone with her and his two servants on the island. Every effort has been bent to give her the most comprehensive education in preparation for a reversal of fortunes which has now been made possible. Miranda is the link connecting the emotional, the spiritual and the political aims of Prospero: she is to be a ruler without paragon. We should not underestimate the importance of his love for her, a concern which makes itself felt most poignantly in his insistence:

> I have done nothing but in care of thee,
> Of thee, my dear one, thee, my daughter.   [I ii 16–17]

But Prospero's well-laid plans go astray. On the failure of his project hinges the weight of academic and dramatic criticism, for we can choose to agree with Kott that the play represents Prospero's (and Shakespeare's) final disillusionment, or with Tillyard and Middleton Murry that, in effecting a 'sea change' on all the characters, the minor disappointments count little in the general mood of euphoria generated by the forgiveness and reconciliation of the final scene.

It is all a matter of what the critic considers Prospero's original aim to have been. Tillyard is unambiguous in stating that Prospero had always intended to pardon his enemies and that he therefore sees his plans fulfilled at the end. But this is to ignore the difficulty Prospero experiences in acting on his principles. His final confrontation with Antonio is painful and harsh:

> For you, most wicked sir, whom to call brother
> Would even infect my mouth, I do forgive
> Thy rankest fault – . . .   [v i 130–2]

These are not the words of a serene magus in control of the situation; it is the confession of a man who has only just discovered that 'the rarer action is in virtue than in vengeance' and who cannot extend this with ease to his usurping brother. Prospero says, immediately after his conversion of vengeance to pity, 'they being penitent, / The sole drift of my purpose doth extend / Not a frown further'. The point is they are *not* all penitent. Sebastian and Antonio remain unchanged by their experiences. When Prospero tells the latter 'I . . . require my dukedom of thee, which, perforce, I know / Thou must restore', the force to which he refers is blackmail. He is only able to make Antonio obey him because of the threat of revealing the recent conspiracy against Alonzo. Kott pithily comments that this avid reader of hermetic books had never studied Machiavelli; but in the end Prospero's 'brave new world' cannot come about without recourse to more sordid political tactics.

Prospero's failure, moreover, goes deeper than this. Fundamentally his art has had no effect whatsoever on the nature of Caliban. Prospero is an idealist, not a realist. Only at the very end does he learn how to be pragmatic. His learning and the exercise of his occult powers make him god-like, but they also make him inhuman. This accounts for his persistent impatience with Miranda and with Ariel: the visionary makes heavy demands on the daughter and the servant. His stronger sense of betrayal on the part of Caliban is a more pronounced dissatisfaction with the real world, a world which Caliban encounters in Trinculo and Stephano and uses to his own ends.

Three times we are made aware of the seer so firmly concentrating on his great projects that he forgets to take into account more mundane matters. His negligence cost him his kingdom when in Milan; it nearly costs Alonzo and Gonzalo their lives; and it returns to plague him at the height of his magical achievement. The plot of Caliban and the clowns is the last straw. Clearly Trinculo and Stephano were no more a part of his original project than was the assassination attempt of Antonio and Sebastian. They represent distractions, yet diversions which nearly prove fatal. We should in no way underestimate the significance of these two unprogrammed twists of the plot, but rather measure the extent of Prospero's ultimate achievement in relation to what he finally learns from them.

Prospero's Agents: (1) Music

In his magical operations Prospero employs Ariel in a variety of functions. By examining these we can observe more clearly the nature and scope of his power. Nature at its most cruel and savage is to be seen during the storm, while the highest manifestation of Prospero's art is the music of Ariel. Always this music leads to a harmony of a personal or political nature. Both these effects spring from the first encounter of the lovers and, moreover, the music has also comforted Ferdinand as it will serve to soothe the other characters later. The actual words sung are never without a deeper significance – notably here in Ariel's song 'Full fathom five' with its reference to 'sea-change' and thus to Prospero's attempt to transform and improve the characters. Music like the sea itself ('Though the seas threaten, they are merciful') is an agent of regeneration.

An idea expressed in *The Merchant of Venice* is most relevant to the significance of music in *The Tempest*. In the earlier play Lorenzo says:

> The man who hath no music in himself,
> Nor is mov'd with concord of sweet sounds,
> Is fit for treasons, stratagems, and spoils;
> The motions of his spirit are as dull as night,
> And his affections dark as Erebus.
> Let no such man be trusted. . . .   [*M. of V.*, v i 83–8]

This concept – pre-Socratic in origin – embraces the notion that the creation of the universe was an imposing of harmony (musical as well as structural) on chaos, and that this harmony, echoed in the music of the spheres, would be perceptible to the human soul were it not for the corrupting effects of sin. At the climactic turning-point of another play, *Pericles*, before being reunited with his wife and daughter, hears the music of the spheres. This allusion is extended in *The Tempest*. Through his art, and chiefly through music, Prospero attempts to affect such a harmony on the worldly plane of politics and human affairs. In Act II scene i, the order in which the political characters fall asleep – thus revealing to what extent they are affected by music and thus in accord with a harmonious universe – is pointed. Gonzalo is the first to yield to the influence, and he is shortly to be followed by all except Alonzo, Antonio and Sebastian. Then, after a short interval, Alonzo accepts the 'heavy offer' of sleep; only Antonio and Sebastian are totally unaffected. They cannot understand the 'strange drowsiness' which possesses the others, any more than they can feel the pangs of conscience. Prospero has significantly underestimated the extent of their evil. His plan was to anaesthetise the whole group; he did not foresee the possibility of two men remaining wholly uninfluenced by his magic. Thus through this scene Shakespeare gives powerful theatrical expression to a basic philosophical and ethical concept.

The inability of the two men who have 'expelled remorse and nature' to yield to the magical and health-giving force of the music is all the more pointedly contrasted with the brute savage's wonderment at hearing the strange harmonies on the island. Nowhere is Caliban more sympathetically presented than when he tells us:

> . . .   the isle is full of noises,
> Sounds, and sweet airs, that give delight and hurt not.

> Sometimes a thousand twangling instruments
> Will hum about mine ears; and sometimes voices
> That, if I had then had wak'd after long sleep,
> Will make me sleep again; and then, in dreaming,
> The clouds methought would open, and show riches
> Ready to drop upon me, that when I waked,
> I cried to dream again.   [iii ii 136–44]

Here nature and art are again juxtaposed in their extremes. Caliban can hear the music and can in his animal way benefit from it: it lulls him to sleep. But it does not affect him more deeply, and he is consequently subject to its appearance and disappearance like a man dreaming. Yet he does recognise its great beauty. His own nature is raw and untamed but not perverted or corrupted as is that of Antonio and Sebastian, who therefore cannot hear the music at all. But Caliban is incapable of comprehending the music and thus of being influenced by it. His appreciation is the open-mouthed wonder of the savage faced with the most beautiful manifestation of a higher art. The 'heavenly music' called up by Prospero 'to work [his] end upon their senses' – and which accompanies the magus's farewell to his art – is of a different order. It is 'A solemn air, and the best comforter / To an unsettled fancy'.

This is a healing music: the characters are united, reborn and soothed by it. It matches the harmony effected on an emotional and political level through the marriage of Ferdinand and Miranda, a union which is celebrated by the dramatic integration of music into the theatrical structure of the masque.

Prospero's Agents: (2) Theatre

It has often been observed that *The Tempest* incorporates many features of the contemporary masque. On Twelfth Night 1605, *The Masque of Blackness* was presented at court. It established a vogue for this new theatrical form: a celebratory, occasional piece which utilised spectacle, music and dance in elaborating a central symbolic and mythical concept or 'device'. *The Masque of Blackness* was a platonic allegory about the power of kingship in which the black nymphs of Niger are 'bleached' by the 'sciential' light of the monarch of the white realm of Albion. It

was written for James's queen, Anne of Denmark, by the
playwright Ben Jonson and staged by the designer Inigo Jones.
Though court masques had flourished in England for many
years, Jones and Jonson revitalised the form in the Stuart
period. Such entertainments were vital to the life of the
Renaissance court. Through their elaboration of symbolic
meanings expressed in visual terms they gave deeper significance to the realities of politics and power. *The Tempest* may well
have served as just such an entertainment: to celebrate the
marriage of the Princess Elizabeth to the Emperor Palatine in
1613. Certainly the 'masque within the masque' reveals
Prospero in the role of 'Presenter', stage managing the
diversion which he has mounted for the benefit of Ferdinand
and Miranda.

With the move by Shakespeare's company, the King's Men,
to the Blackfriars theatre in 1608 there was opportunity for
dramatists to explore the fresh potential of this new theatrical
space. It was indoors, it was more intimate (seating about 700,
unlike the Globe which held up to 3,000) and it catered for a
more select audience. Certain of the new techniques which had
been utilised in the staging of court masques were transferred to
the Blackfriars. Shakespeare's last creative phase was given an
enormous boost by this change of theatrical environment.

What is even more significant is that there is a powerful
connection between the art of Inigo Jones, as architect and
designer, and the occult preoccupations of the age. Jones had
read Dee: notably the preface to Euclid in which the Renaissance idea of the architect is discussed by detailed reference to
the works of Vitruvius. It was Vitruvius who had explained the
laws of perspective in relation to theatrical architecture and
thus paved the way for the theatrical experiments which Jones
was to make in England at the beginning of the seventeenth
century, and which were to effect a radical change on the shape
of the English stage. Hence, as Frances A. Yates puts it:

> In Prospero we may now see, not only the Magus as philosopher
> and as the all-powerful magician ushering in the scientific age
> about to dawn, but also the Magus as creator of the theatre and its
> magic. The immensely rich moment in the history of the theatre in
> which the original power of the actor's theatre is undiminished, but

the imagination is affected by the magic of the masques, finds expression in *The Tempest*.

(Theatre of the World, p. 172)

What Shakespeare discovers in this final play is a powerful theatrical metaphor for expressing his ideas.

Prospero's aims and his failure are to be observed throughout in relation to his skills as a man of the theatre. The storm he conjures up at the beginning of the play is a theatrical effect, but it is in two subsequent scenes that his preoccupations are given even sharper theatrical focus. When he goes to work on the 'three men of sin' Prospero presents them with a trick, a theatrical effect: the disappearing banquet. Ariel's appearance as the Harpy is another of his stage disguises. He confronts the nobles with the consequences of their actions, Prospero's techniques being close to that of Hamlet who presented his play in front of Claudius and Gertrude in the hope that the 'guilty creatures' would 'presently proclaim their malefactions'. The theatre is seen as a powerful agent for changing the world. The entertainment for Miranda and Ferdinand is clearly a masque: it is celebratory, allegorical and it makes its effects through spectacle, song and dance.

Here is the image of the mage as stage-manager, totally in control. But his success is short-lived. Yet again Prospero is seen to be 'Wrapt in secret studies', cut off from the real world. Though powerful enough to engineer this vision he is human enough to forget, and his realisation of this is for him a moment of terror:

Enter certain reapers, properly habited: they join with the Nymphs in a graceful dance towards the end whereof Prospero starts suddenly, and speaks; after which, to a strange, hollow and confused noise, they heavily vanish.

Yet again he has come near to losing his life and sacrificing his daughter. The significance of this event in the drama cannot be too powerfully emphasised. As the stage magic crumbles and the spirit actors disappear, Shakespeare leaves us in no doubt that this is the most terrifying moment in the play.

5   DRAMATIC STRUCTURE AND STYLE

The Three Unities

Shakespeare's experiments in theatrical style at the end of his career were not confined to his adaptation of features from the court masque. *The Tempest* shows an awareness of neo-classical concepts of dramatic form which give precise focus to the complex interrelated themes of the play. The theatrical skill of *The Tempest* resides essentially in Shakespeare's careful compression. All extraneous elements have been eliminated and the remaining material carefully and meaningfully arranged. This compression is achieved in two ways: by concentrating on the final stage of the story, and by observing the neo-classical Unities of Time, Place and Action. A major weakness in each of the three previous romances is the handling of place and time. *Pericles* takes place 'dispersedly in various countries'; *Cymbeline* shifts from England to Italy to Wales; and *The Winter's Tale* alternates between Sicily and Bohemia. A further problem is provided by the necessity of a long gap in time, so that we may see Marina and Perdita both as abandoned babies and young women as well as follow the lengthy story of Imogen's adventures. The devices of Gower and Time as choruses and the clumsy dénouement of *Cymbeline* are all expedients which draw attention to the difficulty of giving to the material of fairy tale and romance a clear theatrical shape.

  The Tempest is the more strikingly original in construction because Shakespeare solved all these theatrical problems simply and ingeniously by focusing on the last stage of the narrative. All the significant action which has both preceded and given rise to Prospero's treatment of the shipwrecked court is conveyed in the long narration of the second scene: a daring dramatic device which could prove tedious were it not handled with great subtlety. Moreover, Prospero makes it clear that speed is vital. Thus the events portrayed both can and must take place within the space of time taken to perform the play. This exact observation of the unity of time further emphasises the theatrical metaphor of the work, drawing attention to Prospero's double role as stage conjurer. We are constantly reminded of the passing of time, notably in the last act where four times [lines 4 136, 186 & 223] reference is made to Prospero's achieving his aims within the allotted three hours.

The Unity of Place is observed in the sense that everything occurs on the same island. It is a 'bare island', reflected in the bare stage of the Globe and Blackfriars theatres, yet a space which can be magically transformed within seconds. The most important of the Three Unities, that of Action, is observed in that all the events on stage are related to Prospero's 'project'. This does not mean that the unforeseen events – the two assassination attempts – were a part of his plan. Rather, his actions are modified by the conduct of others. Aristotle's original insistence on the Unity of Action is a demand for a single plot which determines the development of the whole play. There are no sub-plots in *The Tempest* except in the political rather than the dramatic sense. The scheming of Antonio and Sebastian or of Trinculo and Stephano are variations on the basic theme of the play, mirrors which throw back a disturbing reflection of events which occurred before the play opens. The sense of repetition they impart is a feature which gives the drama added cohesion.

Tragi-comedy

The four romances in general and *The Tempest* in particular represent an attempt to create a new form of drama: pastoral tragi-comedy. The basic theme of pastoral is the contrast of country and court, a theme given fresh emphasis in Shakespeare's confrontation here of nature and nurture. The form of his final play owes a great deal to neo-classical experiments in Italy at the end of the sixteenth century, attempts to define and create a valid third type of drama: tragi-comedy, which was more than a haphazard amalgam of contrasted effects, but rather a careful synthesis of elements from tragedy and comedy in a vital new form with an integrity of its own.

The most important figure in this dramatic renaissance was Giambattista Guarini, whose essay *A Compendium of Tragi-comic Poetry* (published in 1601) and play *The Faithful Shepherd* (published in 1589) served alike to define the form and give it theatrical expression. Guarini's work had a profound effect on some of the young playwrights in England, notably John Fletcher, the rising author who was to take over from Shakespeare as leading dramatist for the King's Men. Fletcher wrote his *The Faithful Shepherdess* as a tribute to the new pastoral genre, and in *Philaster* he created a tragi-comedy which is perfectly within the Guarinian mould. There are strong parallels between *Philaster* and *Cymbeline*, both written at the same time (around 1608), and it comes as no surprise to find Shakespeare collaborating with this newcomer in another tragi-comedy, *The Two Noble Kinsmen*, as well as in *Henry VIII* which was written just after *The Tempest*. Through his association with the younger writer Shakespeare came into close contact with new theatrical ideas from the continent which were to give his drama greater precision and strength.

Guarini's *Compendium* counters the two basic Renaissance arguments against tragi-comedy, defending it as a mixed form and denying that it lacks unity of action. Making analogies with the alloy bronze, and with the hermaphrodite, he claims that tragi-comedy is a valid third dramatic genre, arguing that it is necessary to take precisely what is fitting from the contrasted forms of tragedy and comedy to effect a careful synthesis. He further insists that tragi-comedy should have one basic intrigue, one dénouement and a happy ending which involves all the characters. He goes on to define the function and purpose of this new type of drama which he says seeks 'to imitate through the *mise en scène* a contrived action which combines all the tragic and comic elements which can believably and decorously coexist, regulated within the framework of a unified dramatic form whose aim is to purge with delight the sadness of the audience' (*Compendium*, p. 246).

It is pertinent to ask what was Shakespeare's purpose in writing this play, and we can come much nearer to an appreciation of his intentions through a careful examination of the way in which he has closely observed Guarini's further analysis of precisely how a tragi-comedy should be constructed.

For Guarini each of the five acts of the play has a distinct function in guiding and controlling the audience's response. It is necessary to begin with a pressing issue which determines the pace of the action. In *The Tempest* this is Prospero's 'project',

dependent on its fulfilment in a limited space of time. The first
act must also contrast tragic and comic material so that the
audience is prepared for the mixed genre of the drama as a
whole. This we find in the difference between the violent
opening scene and the consolation of Prospero's subsequent
narration as well as in the meeting of Ferdinand and Miranda
which from the start prepares us for a happy outcome. Act II,
argues Guarini, should introduce new material which is
nevertheless germane to the plot. This is provided by the new
scenes with the court and the clowns, both of which are
concerned with rebellion. Act III should concentrate on comic
plotting with an emphasis on the detailed intrigue which is
proper to comedy rather than tragedy. Here we have Prospero's two designs (on the lovers and on the courtiers) which
fulfil this function, as well as – more tellingly – the dangerous
development of Caliban's plot which occurs between them. Act
IV, in Guarini's scheme, brings the action to its climax, to a
point of greatest tragedy when the characters are most
threatened. Guarini's insistence that the writer of tragi-comedy
take from tragedy 'the danger not the death' is powerfully
realised in *The Tempest* when Prospero's magic collapses with
the recollection of the conspiracy against him. The final act is
concerned with the happy outcome of events: a twist which
should be unexpected yet credible and which involves the
salvation of the virtuous characters and the repentance of the
guilty.

And this is where Shakespeare employs just so much of
Guarini's theory as suits his purpose. It is not the villains who
are repentant in *The Tempest*; it is the hero. This is Shakespeare's most telling dramatic stroke. Nothing has prepared us
for the change of heart in Prospero, yet we accept its
inevitability when we look over the events of the play, both
those which have taken place within these last few hours and
those 'in the dark backward and abysm of time'. Prospero's
conversion has all the theatrical force of the reversal of fortune
and sudden recognition of this on the part of the protagonist
which Aristotle saw as basic to the functioning of tragic
catharsis. The magician's renunciation of his magic, which has
political and aesthetic significance in the context of the major
themes of the play, is charged with meaning and deeply

moving. It is at the same time a gesture of great magnanimity and an act of despair. Prospero can achieve nothing more: his time has run out. And that he should find the confrontation with his old enemies an experience very different from what he had planned is the clearest pointer to Shakespeare's subtle conversion of a dramatic formula into this emotionally complex and ethically ambiguous dénouement.

Theatrical Style

A more detailed analysis of two passages in the play will reveal how Shakespeare's theatrical style functions.

(a) Act I scene ii. Prospero's conversation here with Miranda is the most daring dramatic device, presenting an exposition of complex and crucial past events solely through the form of a long narration, only occasionally (and then briefly) interrupted. This is an immense challenge to the actor, the more so as Prospero is attempting calmly and objectively to give an account of what has happened and yet finds it impossible not to become involved; indeed at times he is carried away by his feelings and responses. This gives the scene a powerful emotional dialectic which is intensified by the bewilderment of Miranda, coming to terms with these devastating revelations and unable to halt her father's flow of words. The pressing issue which Guarini insisted should be basic to the plot is powerfully in evidence in Prospero's further need to make himself clearly and quickly understood. This is a man fighting against time, suddenly confronting his daughter with traumatic revelations and reassuring her that he has everything in control. It is no wonder she falls asleep, exhausted, after a few minutes.

The dialogue opens with Prospero firmly in control. His confident attitude is reflected in the careful balance of the speech, notably at the line 'Which thou heardst cry, which thou saw'st sink' [32]. He begins by probing Miranda with telling questions, rather like a psychiatrist, and then shocks her with the initial revelation – 'Twelve years since, Miranda, twelve year since / Thy father was the Duke of Milan, and / A prince of power' [53] – in which the repetition confirms his confident handling of the situation.

As soon as he starts to describe Antonio, however, his syntax disintegrates under the strain of bitter emotional recollection. The sentence which begins, 'My brother and thy uncle called Antonio' [66], is never completed; he breaks off in a series of parentheses and when he resumes his narrative Antonio is the object of the sentence. Prospero's burning indignation is further expressed in the speech which begins, 'Being once perfected how to grant suits' [79], in which a terse striking image such as 'trash' is followed by a sequence of metaphors which proceed in a stream-of-consciousness manner. The statement that Antonio had 'the key of officer and office' leads through a play on words to the assertion that he 'set all hearts i' the state / To what tune pleased his ear', and is as quickly replaced by the comparison of his brother as 'The ivy which hid my princely trunk' [84–5, 86]. The images here function as they do in contemporary Metaphysical poetry. Prospero's excitement sparks off a mental reaction in which the witty association of ideas fuses emotion and intellect. It needs increasing persistence by Miranda to bring him back to the point, which she does by asking the pertinent questions: 'Wherefore did they not / That hour destroy us?' [138] and 'How came we ashore?' [159]. Hence, after a mere 150 lines, Shakespeare has provided us with the relevant information from the past in such a way as to present Prospero and Miranda vividly before us and through their conversation involve us in the events narrated as well as making us anxious to know how the story will continue.

(b) *Act V scene i*. Prospero's farewell to his art – 'Ye elves of hills, brooks, standing lakes and groves . . .' [33 ff.] – makes an interesting contrast with the above scene and reveals several other characteristic features of the play's style. This is a measured speech of immense rhetorical force, opening with an invocation that expands through seventeen and a half lines without a break. The developing intensity of the verbs employed leads inexorably to the climax of the long invocation. From 'chase', 'fly' and 'rejoice' we move through 'bedimmed' to 'call'd forth', 'set roaring war' and 'given fire', until the powerful physical force of 'rifted', 'made shake' and 'plucked up' explodes in the pile up of 'wak'd', 'op'd' and 'let'em forth' crammed into one line.

Shakespeare is here adapting Golding's translation of

Medea's invocation in Ovid's *Metamorphoses* [VII] which begins: 'Ye Ayres and Windes: ye Elves of Hilles, of Brookes, of Woods alone'. But it is significant that he is closer to the original in such phrases as 'call'd forth' (for Ovid's 'voco') and 'plucked up' (for 'convulsa'). Again, as with his debt to Guarini, Shakespeare takes what he wants from his neo-classical inspiration and adapts it to his own ends. Medea was calling on her gods for assistance; Prospero is invoking his spirits only to relinquish his power over them. The great paragraph which unfolds throughout the first part of the speech – and which taxes to the utmost the vocal resources of the actor – comes to a firm stop at the phrase 'By my so potent Art' [50]. Juxtaposed in the same line is its antithesis: 'But this rough magic'.

The contrast is as powerfully concentrated as that of nature and nurture, and serves as surely to focus our attention on another central theme of the play. As Prospero completes his speech we feel the energy draining out of him; the verbs change to 'break', 'bury' and 'drown', sounding the heavy note of renunciation. And with a telling irony the speech ends with a recollection of Alonzo's determination to seek his son 'deeper than e'er plummet sounded, / And with him there lie mudded' [III iii]. It marks the turning-point in the drama and makes the most complex demands on both audience and actor.

PART TWO: PERFORMANCE

6   INTRODUCTION

The following four productions have been chosen, among
many, for description and comparison as contributing most
usefully, in my opinion, to our understanding of key themes in
The Tempest and of the range of possibility in staging and in the
interpretation of character.

1. The Mermaid Theatre production of 1970, directed by
Jonathan Miller; Graham Crowden as Prospero, Norman
Beaton as Ariel, Randolph Walker as Caliban.

2. The National Theatre production of 1974, directed by
Peter Hall; Sir John Gielgud as Prospero, Michael Feast as
Ariel, Dennis Quilley as Caliban.

3. The Piccolo Teatro production, Milan, of 1978, directed
by Giorgio Strehler and using Agostino Lombardo's translation of the Shakespearean text. Tino Carraro as Prospero,
Giulia Lazzarini as Ariel, Michele Placido and subsequently
Massimo Foschi as Caliban. (Strehler's interpretation has been
shown world-wide on tour by the Piccolo Teatro troupe, as well
as forming part of the Lirico's repertoire in Milan.)

4. The film version, released 1980, directed by Derek
Jarman; Heathcote Williams as Prospero, Karl Johnson as
Ariel, Jack Birkett as Caliban, Toyah Willcox as Miranda.

7   BACKGROUND TO INTERPRETATION:
THE TREATMENT OF ROMANCE

It is fascinating and rewarding to compare two very different
performances of Prospero's speech concerning the renunciation
of his art: that of Sir John Gielgud (recorded on his album *Ages
of Man*: CBS Classics 61830) and that of Heathcote Williams in

the Derek Jarman film (available on a *Palace* video cassette: PVC 2027A). Two more contrasting interpretations it would be difficult to find.

Gielgud brings to the passage the rich musicality and subtlety of poetic inflection for which he is so famous. Beginning the speech in hushed tones deep in the voice, he builds the lines inexorably through a gradual and carefully controlled crescendo which reaches its note of absolute vocal command on the phrase 'By my so potent art'. After a long pause the great organ swell of sound slowly retreats, coming to a final whispered halt. Gielgud's performance represents the assured mastery of a great verse-speaker, sensitively attuned both to the poetry and to the meaning of the passage.

Heathcote Williams delivers the speech in a hoarse bass whisper with little variety of vocal tone or pace. What, for Gielgud, is a rhetorical invocation becomes in Williams's interpretation a brooding passage of introspection. His performance is low-key, more naturalistic – one could say, more modern. He begins, seated, hands on his temples, deeply immersed in an occult text. At one point he turns the page and, just before 'Graves at my command', removes his spectacles. Slowly he looks up from his book and, as he comes to the climactic phrase, 'By my so potent art', he reaches for his staff and gazes into the magic glass which forms part of its structure. His director, Derek Jarman, then cuts from this point straight to the courtiers whom Prospero holds fast in his power. The second part of the speech – the renunciation of 'rough magic' – is omitted.

This is the most striking innovation in a film which is a subtle and challenging reworking of Shakespeare's play. Gielgud's Prospero represents the height of an old acting tradition stretching back to the nineteenth century. It is the tradition of great verse-speaking and of a towering personality dominating the stage. Williams, in contrast, is not first and foremost an actor. He is a writer and performer who through his studies of the occult is also something of a magician himself. With a look he can freeze people in their tracks; he has demonstrated on stage his power to levitate his daughter. Intriguingly, Gielgud is photographed on the cover of the record album in his costume for the National Theatre production of 1974: he is dressed and made up to look like Doctor Dee. But it is Jarman's film which is a much more thorough examination of the occult. His conjurer is a much younger man, a man at the height of his powers. He is a magician whom Jarman sees as successful, no more ready to relinquish his occult strengths than the young director himself is prepared to give up his artistic career.

The Jarman film released in 1980 and Peter Hall's National Theatre production of 1974, with Gielgud playing Prospero for the fourth time in his long career, were totally different in intention and achievement. Hall saw *The Tempest* in terms of the Jacobean court masque and his staging was dominated by equivalents of the theatrical techniques which Inigo Jones introduced into England. The realisation of Ariel (Michael Feast) and Caliban (Dennis Quilley) as concrete visual metaphors was the strongest indication of this.

This spectacular baroque emphasis had a parallel in Giorgio Strehler's production in Milan in 1978. With the actors of Italy's most celebrated and long-established repertory company – the Piccolo Teatro of Milan – Strehler moved into a large theatre (the Lirico) to mount a version of the play which in its overwhelming theatrical force and seriousness of purpose (it ran for four hours) has been acclaimed internationally as the most important Shakespeare production since Peter Brook's famous *A Midsummer Night's Dream* in 1970.

The fourth subject of detailed analysis is very different. In 1970 Jonathan Miller directed a highly unorthodox production at the Mermaid Theatre in which, doing away entirely with any effects of visual stage magic, he concentrated instead on the theme of colonisation in the play. Casting black actors (Norman Beaton and Randolph Walker respectively) in the roles of Ariel and Caliban, and having Graham Crowden play Prospero as a tough local governor, he went straight to the heart of the debate on nature and nurture, illuminating it with penetrating new insights and in so doing relating the drama closely to modern ethical and political issues.

I have chosen these four contrasted examples carefully and deliberately. *The Tempest* is – of all Shakespeare's plays – the one most often considered a great poetical work, yet lacking in drama, its theatrical effects frequently dismissed as superficial and incidental. As well as being a great poet Shakespeare absorbed all the major cross-currents of contemporary thought and gave his ideas precise and vivid shape on the stage. The literary bias of academic criticism has for centuries impeded a thorough examination of his plays as drama and theatre. As Kott has sought to remind us, Shakespeare is our contemporary; only by moving from theory to practice in staging the plays can his ideas come into meaningful contact with ours. A play does not exist until it takes shape in the theatre. Kott has also pointed out that *The Tempest* is the most Italian of Shakespeare's works. The names of the characters, their background, the setting (on an island just off the route from Tunis to Naples in the same location as that on which Aeneas was shipwrecked when undertaking the same journey), and the debt to the Commedia dell'Arte in the scenes of clowning – all make it appropriate that this study should include an outstanding Italian production.

More conservative critics feel that the sanctity of the text is violated both by the imposition of non-theatrical criteria, such as Miller's social and anthropological viewpoint, or Jarman's version which, as well as cutting over half the lines and radically transposing most of the rest, relies on highly unorthodox casting (for example, Toyah Willcox as Miranda, Jack Birkett as Caliban, Karl Johnson as Ariel). But it is more important to ask whether the ends justify the means. It is salutary to note that Peter Hall is the only one of the four directors who has not expressed the feeling that *The Tempest* occupies a very special place in his work. His production and Gielgud's performance were relatively conventional; they stand as touchstones against which the other, more ambitious, alternatives may be judged.

It is important that these four productions be seen in the context of the stage-history of the play, itself a chronicle of adaptation and distortion of Shakespeare's original. The Revels Accounts for the year 1611 record a performance – presumably the first – of *The Tempest*. Two years later it was acted before the Princess Elizabeth and the Elector Palatine, serving as the perfect entertainment to celebrate their marriage. Thereafter the play as Shakespeare wrote it was little performed until this century, for the version by Dryden and Davenant (first performed at the Duke's Theatre, Lincoln's

Inn Fields on 7 November 1667) held the stage in preference to the original. By giving Miranda a younger sister, Dorinda, and a male counterpart in Hippolyto (a youth who had never seen a woman), and by creating a female monster, Sycorax, as well as a female sprite, Milcha, the authors elaborated the play beyond recognition and provided a drama in tune with Restoration taste, as well as suiting the vogue for spectacle which was to develop through the next two centuries. In 1673 or 1674, this version was turned into an opera with music by Purcell and produced by Shadwell at the rival Dorset Gardens Theatre. These two travesties of the original influenced the stagings by the leading actor-managers of the next two centuries, from Garrick and Kemble through to Phelps and Charles Kean.

Earlier this century the play was still not taken very seriously as the amusing comments of the wry iconoclastic critic James Agate make clear. In reviewing Charles Laughton's performance on 8 January 1934, Agate – confessing to an impatience with the play and calling Prospero 'that endless chunderer' – avowed that the protagonist reminded him of Father Christmas who 'performed his hocus pocus with a naughty little twinkle in his eye'. More significantly, Agate reviewed the comparatively recent stage-history of the play, informing us that: 'As for the Benson troupe, their distinguished old chief used to hang by his toes from the tops of poplars, leaving Prospero to be played by the stick engaged for Duncan, or anybody else over eighty' (*Brief Chronicles*, p. 17). 'I never heard of Irving playing Prospero', he adds. 'Presumably he had more sense.'

Beerbohm Tree, the great Shakespearean actor-manager at the turn of the century, also chose to play Caliban. Critics remarked that the savage had become the principal character. *The Times* commented that he was so grand and grotesque that he swamped the lovers and Prospero alike. Tree cut the epilogue, ending instead with a vision of the ship sailing away leaving Caliban firmly centre-stage, shading his eyes to catch a final glimpse of the boat transporting a civilisation he humbly worshipped. This is a far cry from the modern productions which are more critical of that civilisation and more complex in their portrayal of the native.

It is in the context of an essentially nineteenth-century tradition that we should see Gielgud's first and second interpretations of Prospero. He first played the part at the Old Vic in 1930 in a production directed by Harcourt Williams. The décor was 'Persian-cum-Japanese'. He had been told by the great Russian director, Komisarjevsky, that he ought not to wear a beard and should look like Dante: 'I did', remarked Gielgud, 'with a turban.' Harcourt Williams later wrote: 'Prospero, who is usually made into a dull old boy by most actors, in John's sensitive hands became a being of great beauty' (*Old Vic Saga*, p. 95). The production by George Devine and Marius Goring at the same theatre ten years later marked Gielgud's second attempt at the part of Prospero. This time, instead of the 'turbanned eastern conjurer' he played the part as 'a cross old gentleman', ascetic, irrascible and robed like a priest. The directors wanted a vigorous Prospero still at the height of his powers and full of passion for life. His decision to renounce his magic thus took on an added significance. Gielgud has made the part very much his own, developing and deepening his interpretation over the years. From the rather nebulous shape of his first benevolent Prospero he has gradually explored the tensions and misgivings in the character so as to make him an altogether more dramatically complex and interesting figure. Through his successive assumptions of the part he has been instrumental in bringing about a revaluation of the play: a consideration of its serious themes as against an attitude to the work as an escapist romance dressed up in exotic trimmings and offering an opportunity for spectacular theatrical pyrotechnics.

A world of difference separates the two earlier productions from the later ones. In 1957 Gielgud again played Prospero, this time in the Peter Brook staging at Stratford. He attempted to look like a figure from an El Greco painting, half-naked above the waist and wearing sandals. Brook had suggested the idea of a hermit and Gielgud developed this into the figure of a biblical anchorite with cropped greying hair. Brook's conception of the work as first and foremost a revenge play, and Gielgud's presentation of the agony of a tortured saint, were innovative and influential. The drama escaped entirely from the romantic associations of the Harcourt Williams concept or the Devine/Goring production with its misty and mysterious scenery by Oliver Messel which gave the impression of the action taking place at the bottom of the sea. This was the first time Brook had staged the play; he too has returned to it twice since. It holds a particular fascination for him, and in *The Empty Space* he discusses it in terms of its unique position in the Shakespearean canon:

> When we realise that it takes place on an island and not on an island, during a day and not during a day, with a tempest that sets off a series of events that are still within a tempest, even when the storm is done, that the charming pastoral naturally encompasses rape, murder, conspiracy; when we begin to unearth the themes that Shakespeare has so carefully buried, we see that it is his complete final statement and that it deals with the whole condition of man. (*The Empty Space*, pp. 95–6)

This approach to the play as a work of great ambiguity and significance was extended in the Stratford production of 1963 in which Clifford Williams collaborated with Peter Brook on the direction. Williams pushed the implications of Brook's thesis further:

> The play is termed a romance, but you can't present a romance in romantic terms – the baroque, the rococo; we don't respond to them any more. Romance in that sense is a lie about life; fairy tales exclude all the messy, inevitable facts of the world . . . if there is any reconciliation at the end, there is infinitely more irresolution. . . . A man spends his life trying to perfect his responses to the world, to control himself and nature; he still ends up senile. In this play Shakespeare includes all the themes from his earlier work – kingship, inheritance, treachery, conscience, identity, love, music, God; he draws them together as if to find the key to it all, but there is no such key. There is no grand order and Prospero returns to Milan not bathed in tranquillity, but a wreck.
>
> (Quoted in J. C. Trewin, *Peter Brook*, p. 135)

This interpretation – despite a powerful central performance from Tom Fleming – did not meet with critical approval. It was perhaps too bleak in its conclusions, more uncompromising than Brook's 1957 production with Gielgud. It had to wait for Peter Hall in 1974 to take up two of the issues raised by Clifford Williams's comments: the suggestion of the appropriateness of a baroque staging and the strong sense of failure on Prospero's part.

Brook returned to the play in 1968 in an experimental production at the Roundhouse. This version, commissioned by the French director Jean-Louis Barrault, brought together players from France, Britain, Japan and the United States to explore theatrical techniques of expression. For the opening storm, for instance, a Japanese actor crouched vocalising sounds of wind and terror whilst the rest huddled together whimpering and trembling. It was an investigation of certain themes of the play, essentially mounted as an exercise for actors. It was, however, to bear fruit in many of Brook's subsequent productions, most notably his celebrated *Midsummer Night's Dream* in 1970.

8 NATURE/NURTURE: COLONISATION

It is not surprising that Beerbohm Tree and Benson should have chosen to play Caliban; he is in many ways the most ambiguous and sympathetic character in the play. In all four of the productions we shall now examine in detail how he has been brought to powerful theatrical life, and in a marked variety of ways. In order to convey his essentially contradictory characteristics, both Strehler and Hall presented him in a physically two-fold manner.

In Hall's 1974 production, Dennis Quilley's interpretation of the part received unanimously ecstatic notices from the critics. His make-up was bisected: one half of his face presented the ugly deformed monster, the other an image of the noble savage. This meant that, in visual terms, by turning his profile to the audience he could change his appearance in a moment. Hall employed this device – one perfectly consistent with his emphasis on visual symbolism in the manner of Inigo Jones – to subtle effect, often counterpointing Caliban's appearance with his words and with the action on stage. The rich associations of Hiawatha and the Last of the Mohicans were thus able to force the central issue of the conflict of nature and nurture firmly into the audience's visual and intellectual perception.

Strehler, in his Milan (1978) production, worked in a

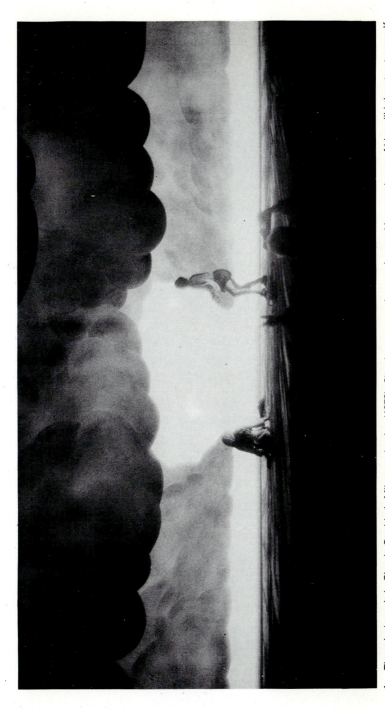

1. Theatrical magic in Giorgio Strehler's Milan production (1978). Clouds appear and waves (created by vast sheets of blue silk) threaten to engulf the lovers (Fabiana Udenio and Massimo Bonetti) as Prospero (Tino Carraro) remembers the 'foul conspiracy'. Photo: Luigi Ciminaghi

2. Ariel (Giulia Lazzarini) – a white-faced Pierrot with the grace of a ballerina – hovers above Prospero in Strehler's production. Photo: Luigi Ciminaghi

3. (*main picture*): Ariel (Michael Feast) — spirit clinging to a slim bone — in Peter Hall's 1974 National Theatre production, influenced by the masque designs of Inigo Jones. Prospero (John Gielgud) is costumed and made up to resemble the Elizabethan magus, Doctor John Dee. By contrast to Carraro, Gielgud never looked directly at his servant, thus establishing Ariel as an extension of Prospero's mind. Photo: Zoë Dominic (*inset*): Derek Jarman's Ariel (Karl Johnson) in his 1980 film, recalling Jan Kott's description: 'a laboratory assistant working at an atomic reactor'. Photo: courtesy of Boyd's Co., London.

4a. The unconventional pair of lovers (Toyah Willcox and David Meyer) in the Jarman film. Photo: courtesy of Boyd's Co., London.

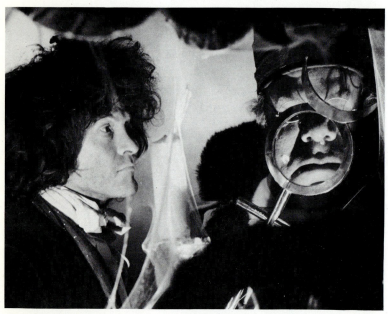

4b. Prospero (Heathcote Williams) holds Alonzo (Peter Bull) 'spell-stopped' by the use of his magic wand modelled on Doctor Dee's hieroglyphic monad. Photo: courtesy of Boyd's Co., London.

somewhat different manner. Again, the make-up of Caliban – at a certain stage in the play – was divided. One side of his face became covered in war-paint after the first confrontation with Prospero while the other remained clear. He was portrayed as a black native by a white actor whose physicality was powerfully emphasised. On his first appearance (from a trap in the stage floor) his cursing was complemented by a crouching animal posture which further stressed his brute nature. But when Prospero ordered him to work, Caliban raised himself to his full height, stepped back and looked his master straight in the eye. He immediately became a handsome boy with a beautiful figure and, as he glared at Prospero with wide open eyes, the impression was of a noble innocent cruelly oppressed by a tyrannical overseer. As he turned and slowly walked off-stage his majestic bearing made Prospero, his belt raised threateningly, seem the true savage.

Derek Jarman's Caliban in his 1980 film production is the blind mime-actor, Jack Birkett, better known as The Great Orlando in his partnership with Lindsay Kemp. He is in every sense a grotesque figure: bald, shambling, displaying in grisly close-up his ugly teeth set in a permanent grimace of hatred. Yet his Caliban is irresistibly pathetic despite his ugly appearance, though it would be counter to Jarman's emphasis on the benign and all-powerful magic of Prospero to present the slave in such a way as to discredit the master. A striking shot early in the film establishes his repulsive bestial nature which at the same time retains an intense fascination. We see him breaking a raw egg with his teeth and sucking out the contents with noisy relish. His danger is very considerably toned down. Instead of being afraid of him, Miranda sees him as a figure of fun, throwing a sponge at him and kicking him out of the room when he disturbs her taking a bath. His plot against Prospero is never any real threat: Trinculo and Stephano have already met up and are blind drunk when we first see them. By contrast, Caliban's attempts to make them stick to their plan are the more pathetically ineffective and his ultimate recognition of the folly of his ways more credible.

The issues hinted at in the presentation of Caliban by Strehler and Hall assumed a central focus in Jonathan Miller's production (1970). Miller felt that Caliban was monstrous for those who had never seen such people – just as, for Miranda (who had never seen civilised life), it was a 'brave new world' that confronted her at the end of the play. The two are complementary pictures of one another. Miller argued that, if you examine the anthropology of the sixteenth and seventeenth centuries, you will find that the response to primitive peoples was that they were in some way deformed, peculiar or degenerate versions of men.

Prospero's magic was seen in this production as a very real power: the power of the white conqueror of a black continent. Thus Miller presented both Ariel and Caliban as black slaves: the one a dignified butler, the other a grinning field-hand in an ill-fitting greatcoat. The critic Ronald Bryden saw Ariel as the Uncle Tom and Caliban as the black rebel, but Miller explained the distinction rather differently:

> You get two forms of tribal response to the white colonials – either a detribalised, broken-down, shuffling, disinherited feeling – which is what Caliban represents – or, on the other hand, a sophisticated technologically-capable, fast-learning response which was represented by the Ibus in Nigeria who were capable of picking up all the administrative skills whilst still pressing for their liberty.*

Miller's starting-point for his production was an anthropological study: *Prospero and Caliban* by Otto Manonet. Believing firmly that the philosophical content of Shakespeare's plays is of prime importance, Miller is a director who profoundly mistrusts a reliance simply on theatrical sources. His thesis was that the play represents the tragic and inevitable disintegration of a more primitive culture as the result of European invasion and colonisation. Prospero's effect he saw as essentially deleterious, 'disinheriting those who know they have a close connection with nature. After the departure of the white master, thorough detribalisation and the elaborate sophistication of the white culture are then set firmly at each other's throats.' The production ended with the provocative picture of Caliban shaking his fist at the disappearing ship while Ariel picked up Prospero's staff and began to straighten it.

Miller was able to bring out very strongly the irritable

---

* All quotations by Jonathan Miller are taken from an interview with the present author, 22 September 1983.

dictatorial aspect of Prospero, and link the different strands of the plot to his over-all idea. The debate on the commonwealth assumed the importance it merits, and the political scenes had an edge lacking in many other versions of the play. The masque was presented in terms of black inhabitants seconded to Prospero's intentions and sung by black actresses. The comic scenes also came into focus in a vivid original way. Miller based them on the image of British private soldiers in Port Said making the natives drunk, patronising them and bullying them. 'It is what army sergeants and NAAFI corporals always do when they arrive in a foreign country', he remarked. 'They shout loudly at the people to make them understand, make them drunk and then get drunk themselves. I had modern NCO's in mind but I'm sure it must have been how European sailors behaved in the sixteenth century.' It certainly made what can often seem the most tiresome comic scenes in Shakespeare at the same time richly funny and disturbingly serious.

9   MAGIC AND PERFORMANCE

The way in which a director chooses to present the theme of colonisation in the play will inevitably affect his approach to the supernatural. Miller's production was attacked by some rather shallow critics as lacking, grace, beauty and magic. His reply to this was that magic is the interior of the mind; it is not represented adequately by a 'bag of tricks' on the stage. What fascinates Miller is the magic of science. He saw Prospero as 'a man who had studied not merely the occult subjects but the occult subjects in connection with science'. He pointed to Frances Yates's revelation that the Royal Society was partly rooted in the Rosicrucian movement, from which one sees that at the time Shakespeare was writing *The Tempest* the occult and the scientific were inter-related. This is reflected perfectly sixty years later in the character of Isaac Newton whose more famous discoveries concerning gravity represented only a fraction of his research, which was devoted equally to determining the dating of the Flood and to formulating a theory of colours. Miller saw Prospero as a figure midway between Doctor Dee and Newton and set his production at a time precisely contemporary with the play.

Graham Crowden's Prospero in this production more closely resembled the scientist than the conjurer. He accompanied the singers in the masque at a desk organ. This was not the grand organiser of magical apparitions; as one critic commented, he would have been equally at home with a quadrant or a harpsichord. Miller wished to get away from the commonplace view of magic which is accepted in the theatre. When the court are presented with the feast [III iii], he saw this as a hallucination. The characters stared into the audience in a mesmerised sort of way, started to tuck bibs into their collars and to salivate when confronted by a meal that was not there. This forced the audience to use their imagination, a technique perhaps more proper to the bare public stage of the Globe than the indoor theatre at the Blackfriars which was able to exploit the use of spectacular visual effects. Irving Wardle was particularly impressed by the staging of this scene:

> Take the episode of the magical feast. Instead of the apparition of the harpy and parade of spectral waiters in cornucopian headgear, Norman Beaton as Ariel descends on a bare stage, slow-moving and dignified as ever in his black costume; while the courtiers stare in amazement at a vision above the audience, stretch out their hands and freeze. This is a true invocation to theatrical magic.
>
> (*The Times*, 16 June 1970)

The emphasis on the scientific nature of occult power strongly echoed Jan Kott's comments on Prospero's renunciation of his art:

> Prospero's soliloquy (in Act v) . . . is closest to Leonardo's enthusiasm for the power of the human mind which has wrenched from nature her elemental forces. . . . Every age interprets the soliloquy through its own experience. To us it is an atomic soliloquy, and there is in it awe rather than enthusiasm. . . . We hear in this soliloquy an apocalyptic tone. It is not however the poetic Apocalypse of the romantics, but the Apocalypse of nuclear explosions and the atomic mushroom.
>
> (*Shakespeare Our Contemporary*, pp. 199–200)

Harold Hobson's review of the production underlined this aspect of Miller's interpretation:

> By one of the paradoxes of art the play becomes most magical when magic is about to depart from it. Graham Crowden does not deliver the speech about 'cloud-capped towers' and 'gorgeous palaces' as the customary glacial display of verbal virtuosity; he makes it rather as a man who looks into the future and sees their destruction and the destruction of the great globe itself with a shuddering fear. The baroque beauty of the verse is strengthened with human emotion so that when he comes to Prospero's renunciation of his supernatural powers he presents to us the figure of a man who is giving up an empire without the cover of which he will be unable to establish any real contact with his fellow-beings. . . . Mr Crowden's is a Prospero who is unequal to equality, which makes the nobility of surrender all the greater. Mr Miller's discovery that his supernaturalism is founded on a natural insufficiency makes Prospero for the first time not only an interesting but a sympathetic, even heroic figure.
>
> (*Sunday Times*, 21 June 1970)

Miller had Graham Crowden deliver this speech with power visibly draining out of him; at the end he lay curled up on the ground, his body resembling a helpless foetus.

When asked how it might be possible to represent on stage the sort of magic associated with Cornelius Agrippa and Doctor Dee, Miller replied that it would be very difficult to make that type of occult power tangible and credible. The medium of film – with sudden intercutting of shots, quick fades and dissolves – lends itself far more readily to such an approach.

This is exploited to stunning effect in Derek Jarman's cinematic version. Jarman actually believes in magic. His library is crammed with occult literature from Agrippa through Dee to Frances Yates, and for him Prospero is first and foremost a Renaissance magus. All the magic in his film was accurate: the signs and symbols chalked on the walls were copied from cabalistic documents; the text Prospero is poring over when he begins his invocation is the first English edition of Cornelius Agrippa; the conjurer possesses a wand and optic glass which take the form of Dee's hieroglyphic monad, the symbol of unity in the world. Jarman was concerned to create a powerful mood which would establish from the start a magical atmosphere. He did this by filming the work on location at Stoneleigh Abbey. Feeling that the problem with Shakespearean film settings is that they are often too realistic and fight with the descriptive power of the verse, he chose a more abstract approach. The action does not take place on a bare island but rather in what he has described as a 'Chinese box' situation in which the events move inside the house. He used the burnt-out, half-ruined eighteenth-century wing of the crumbling abbey, originally built in the mid sixteenth century. The house imposed a certain atmosphere on the film, a mysterious romantic mood which Jarman carried through in the mixture of periods in the costumes. Caliban is a late nineteenth-century butler, Ariel a modern worker, Prospero a run-down Beethoven; some of the spirits are dressed as figures from a Velázquez painting.

Heathcote Williams was chosen to play Prospero because he shares Jarman's interest in the occult. 'Heathcote *was* Prospero as opposed to acting him', his director commented, adding:

> You have to believe in the magic; it always looks unreal – theatrical in the worst sense – on stage and never works. Heathcote can do those silly sort of ordinary magical things that happen in the play: disarm people just by looking at them for example. He can make you believe he has this power. Hence it was possible to get away from base magic and concentrate on real magic – which is obviously in the mind.*

Jarman sees the significance of magic as deeply political. Shakespeare, strongly influenced by Dee, was, he feels, making a statement about the superiority of Renaissance values – learning, rediscovery of the arts, scientific exploration – over the reactionary attitude which dominated the new century when James I came to the throne. James's mistrust of the occult expressed itself in his persecution of witchcraft: a far cry from Elizabeth who employed Dee to cast the horoscope for her coronation. Jarman sees a contemporary parallel in all this, one explored in his previous film *Jubilee* which contrasts the reigns of the two Elizabeths and in a final shot shows Dee walking through the devastation of the modern world. Jarman is a

---

* Detailed information on this 1980-released film version is taken from the present author's interview with Derek Jarman, 16 July 1983.

product of the freedom and spirit of enquiry which characterised the English cultural scene in the 1960s and 1970s. His film – and his representation of magic as an intellectual and imaginative faculty of the utmost significance – is a stand against the puritanism and conservatism which have developed here in the last decade.

Jarman's Prospero is virtually omnipotent. He does not reject his magic. He has no reason to do so; it has served him well and achieved all his aims. The final vision of the film – the ruined stately home with the broken-down aristocrat and the unwilling worker – is a metaphor for England. Ariel escapes as Prospero is dreaming; he is not given his freedom. Karl Johnson's Ariel is a thoroughly modern creation. Pale-faced, with short cropped hair and dressed in a boiler suit, he is the technician for his master's experiments. There is more than a hint of Kott's description of the character as resembling 'a laboratory assistant working at an atomic reactor'. Caliban's significance in the context of black and white magic is extended by showing us Sycorax in a brief flash-back which presents her as an obese, naked sorceress, heavily made up and smoking a hookah. Her association with the exotic world of North Africa is thus emphasised, as is her viciousness in tormenting Ariel to the sadistic delight of her son.

Both the plot against Alonzo and Caliban's plan to kill Prospero are firmly in the magician's control: the scene of the attempted assassination is heavily cut and Prospero does not forget the 'foul conspiracy'. The masque which celebrates the betrothal of Ferdinand and Miranda is a very different affair from that Shakespeare envisaged. Jarman's magic wittily conjures up Elizabeth Welch, accompanied by a crowd of very unorthodox mariners, to sing 'stormy weather'. Again, the director's politics – here his sexual politics – transform Shakespeare's presentation of a celebratory masque which crumbles at the onset of reality into a modern statement on the difficulty of believing that marriage is an institution which inspires absolute faith.

10   PROSPERO'S AIMS

The most basic question any actor playing Prospero and any
director mounting the play must ask himself is: What precisely
is the magician's aim? From this will stem the related issue of
the extent to which he realises this aim, to what extent his
project is successful.

It is regrettable that one of the few essays on the theatrical (as
distinct from the literary and dramatic) problems of the play
should be so wrong-headed. David William has written what
promises to be an analysis of the play in terms which relate to
the actor and director (see Reading List, below). He goes
straight to the heart of the matter by discussing Prospero's plan
in relation to Stanislavsky's theory, pointing out that the actor
should see his motivation in terms of the 'creative objective'
which governs his conduct. Unfortunately, at this point his
analysis is invalidated through a simple but fundamental
misunderstanding of Stanislavsky. The Russian director
argued that an actor's performance is given purpose and clarity
by being split into various units which determine the scope of
his aims and desires. His ultimate dominating urge is his
super-objective: the basic controlling end of all his endeavours. In
order to achieve this he attempts to fulfil a series of *objectives*,
each of which contributes to the overall plan. These too are
broken down into smaller, more immediate *intentions* which –
directly or indirectly – further his plans.

The Tempest offers a perfect illustration of the attempt to
realise a related series of aims. Prospero's super-objective is the
handing over of Naples and Milan to the joint heirs, Ferdinand
and Miranda. His particular objectives, therefore, are essentially the bringing together of the lovers and the attempt to
make the guilty restore to him his rightful inheritance. To
achieve this he employs a variety of actions – bullying,
terrifying, obstructing, even blackmailing – which individually
advance his plan one stage further. David William, in his
shallow reading of Stanislavsky, observes that the objective
should be seen in terms of an infinitive, but utterly misses the
vital point, both in Stanislavsky's method and in the play itself,
by defining this as 'to pardon the deceiver'.

Stanislavsky's most important concern was that the actor should conceive of his objectives and intentions in terms of concrete finite actions. To bully, to terrify, to make the guilty repent, to regain his dukedom, are actions an actor can *play*; to forgive is passive and will not sustain a performance or give it purpose. It is just such a nebulous dominating concern which leads to the worst sort of interpretations of Prospero: that of Charles Laughton in 1934, which Agate said had 'a face cherubically set against spirits which may turn out to be evil'; or that of Alistair Sim in the early 1960s, which made the revengeful magus into a bumbling benign schoolmaster. Prospero has absolutely no intention of pardonning the deceiver when he initiates his project. It is his change of heart – and of plans – consequent upon the measure of failure in their realisation which gives the play its dramatic conflict and theatrical force. Prospero's aims are very specific, and he employs his magic in a scientific way to achieve them. It is magic with very clear limitations and he is a man engaged in a race against time.

The development in Gielgud's performances from 1930 to 1974 reveals a movement from generalised beneficence towards a painful, difficult change of heart. It is a development which has enriched the characterisation through a sharper definition of intentions. Gielgud's tetchy Prospero of 1940, a man more removed from life and thus a colder figure than that of 1930, was also stronger, more determined. In the Brook production of 1957 this developed into a man bent first and foremost on revenge who is gradually convinced that hatred and vengeance are useless. The magus was also taking clearer shape as a Baconian figure aware that man commands nature by obeying her. This Prospero was a hard man, manifesting little kindness or parental affection and taking little joy in his magical powers. The contemporary critic for *The Times* concluded that he was 'an angry and embittered aristocrat speaking his tortured thoughts as though they disgusted him'. Brook gave the governing super-objective vivid physical life at the climax of the play by transforming the stage into the ship bound for Naples with Prospero triumphantly at the helm.

Peter Hall's National Theatre production of 1974 explored even further the character's careful ruthless plotting. Disliking

the traditional interpretation of Prospero as 'an aesthetic
schoolmaster who was thinking of higher things', he saw him as
'a man of power, of intelligence, as shrewd and cunning and
egocentric as Churchill' (*Peter Hall's Diaries*, ed. John Goodwin,
p. 12). Hall was concerned that Gielgud, despite his performance in the Brook production, would be 'too gentle and too
nice', and was confident he could push him into 'a harsher
area of reality'. He further particularised the problem which
emerged in rehearsal (p. 76):

> [Prospero's] passion for revenge is not emotional but puritanical.
> John shows the agony that Prospero is going through from the very
> beginning of the play. He should wait until the end. Macbeth has to
> be played by an actor who is content to act dangerously little for the
> first half of the play. The technique is the same with Prospero.
> Except that Prospero must wait until three quarters of the play is
> over until he gets emotional – in the masque.

In the event Gielgud did hold his emotional and rhetorical
punches until he witnessed the near-destruction of his project, a
realisation that enraged him both because of the evil of his
adversaries and his own guilty neglect of the danger.

There remained, however, one fundamental and significant
aspect of Gielgud's 1974 performance which hindered his real
success in conveying the harsh concept of the failed magician.
The great tradition of verse speaking which he represents – and
which we can hear on his recording of the speech of renunciation – is inimical to such an interpretation. Gielgud did a great
deal to avoid the 'singing' and 'emoting' which was counter to
Hall's concept of the character, delivering 'Our revels now are
ended' on a savage rather than a lyrical note. But in a basic
sense his vocal skills were something of a hindrance in the role.
The careful organisation of the poetic effects makes it difficult
to believe in any spontaneous reaction to events. Harold
Hobson's response to the production, though extreme, underlined the problem, making it clear that a playgoer, tuned to the
cadences of the powerful verse speaker, always finds it difficult
to hear what is new and is quick to reject what he senses as
antipathetic in the reading: 'No monstrosity can disturb the
calm flow of Gielgud's musical delivery, which floats on like the
majestic Oxus, untouched by frosty starlight, or Polar star, or

the hushed Charasmian waste: detached, and blessedly making the rest of the production irrelevant' (*Sunday Times*, 10 March 1974). It is fascinating to consider what Olivier, whom Hall originally wanted for the role, would have made of it.

Hobson was very sensitive, however – as we have seen – to Jonathan Miller's less sympathetic conception of Prospero in his 1970 production. In fact, Miller's first choice for the part had also been another actor, Michael Hordern, who had played Lear for him previously. But Hordern found the colonisation thesis unattractive and wanted to play Prospero as a more likeable figure. (This he was able to do later, both at Stratford and on television.) In the event, a starker production than Hall's, with a less mellifluous leading actor, came much nearer to achieving a revaluation of the play and a clarification of Prospero's basic objective. It could be argued that he is concerned to get his own back and to punish his enemies: aims which can be seen both in a negative and a positive light. The tyrannical local governor – the figure presented by Graham Crowden in the Miller production – forced the negative aspect of the project more clearly to the fore. Because the director was more concerned with Prospero's deleterious effect on the island, his political achievement in respect of Naples and Milan was seen in a more critical light. Miller was clear, however, that Prospero has 'an elaborate project of tuition'; he teaches the miscreants the wrongness of their ways. It is an accident that they have come within his power and he has not programmed the attempt on Alonzo's life. But, Miller argued, 'though it causes him trouble it works to his advantage in the end. It substantiates his suspicions. He needs to have their wickedness demonstrated.' This approach more fully underlined Prospero's resort to blackmail as the means to force his brother to obey him.

Another important aspect in the direction of the play is the handling of Prospero's relationship with Miranda. If this is not firmly and powerfully established from the start, and is not consistently evident in his behaviour throughout, there is a real danger of losing sight of the super-objective which is intimately bound up with his concern for his daughter's welfare. The major weaknesses of Hall's 1974 production was the presentation of the lovers and the lack of any feeling that Prospero's plan began and ended with his daughter. The opposite was the case with Miller's staging. He explained:

> The sequestration of daughter and father on an island which in fact, up until the moment of the arrival of the ship-wrecked passengers, is apparently impenetrable to the outside world with all its corruptness of 'who's in, who's out', is absolutely like Lear's vision of what he and Cordelia will do in the gilded cage of their prison. It's like Lear's dream. It's what he would have liked to have done.

This subtle parallel with the earlier and seminal tragedy was realised in the intense concern Crowden's Prospero showed for his frail bewildered daughter and extended in the scenes in which he watched her growing love as she and Ferdinand awoke to a new awareness of their bodies and feelings.

Toyah Willcox's performance in Derek Jarman's film version serves the more clearly to focus our attention on the better life which Prospero makes possible through his powers. Heathcote Williams's magician is altogether more successful, the complete realisation of his plans serving to clarify his initial objective. The 'spell-stopped' court and the bedraggled grotesquely costumed fools, who are literally frozen in their tracks, are released to share in the celebration of the lovers' betrothal. Alonzo is overjoyed; and Prospero's confrontation with his brother is reduced to a curt monosyllable on the part of Antonio as he acknowledges his total defeat. Miranda's delight at the masque is the reaction to a brave new world into which she has slowly grown. Jarman expands the awareness of Miranda's love for Ferdinand by showing her gradually emerge as a more adult figure. She is first seen as a frightened child, cowering in bed; subsequently she kisses her rocking-horse goodbye – a poignant image for her rejection of childhood; and she is later seen alone putting on airs and graces in an amusing attempt to assert her newly-discovered status as a princess. She is entirely her father's child: her off-beat unkempt appearance and her evident sensuality are the inevitable corollary of his dishevelled intensity and physical vitality.

11   THEATRICAL SPECTACLE

Giorgio Strehler's magician had a very different aim in mind. In the Milan production (1978) he was essentially a man of the theatre, and the Italian director employed his conjuring skills as a metaphor for the power of art in general and theatre in particular to change the world. This meant that Prospero's objectives were seen in terms of stage effects which had a necessarily limited efficacity. The love of Ferdinand and Miranda did not elicit any undue surprise on the line 'It works!' Nor was Prospero thrown emotionally off-balance by the realisation that he had forgotten the conspiracy against him. Indeed, Strehler cut the celebratory masque, the more to emphasise the previous apparition of Ariel as the harpy: an interruption which by contrast is intended to have a profound effect on the spectators. This interpretation emphasised the autobiographical element in the play and minimised both the threats to Prospero and the necessity to act urgently. A production lasting – as this did – for four hours was little concerned with the magician's temporal limitations.

The strength of the concept resided in the theatrical force of Strehler's stage images. This was the absolute antithesis of Miller's approach. It placed the emphasis on theatrical magic, but was more than an empty display of stunning effects. The director made the theme of his version the exploration of the nature and power of the stage. It became an analysis of the artist's responsibility as well as an examination of Shakespeare's concern to explore and justify his craft. Strehler has argued:

> Here at the heart of *The Tempest* the man of the theatre finds himself face to face with theatre in its ultimate reality. He reaches, or thinks he reaches, the furthest limits of theatre. In *The Tempest* there is the extreme weariness and vanity of the theatre, yet at the same time the glorification of theatre and of life. The illusory and triumphant glorification of theatre as the noblest means of imparting knowledge and teaching history; but an awareness that it is a limited medium, one always unable in the last analysis to capture the indefinable workings of life itself.*

* This and the following excerpt are from an article by Giorgio Strehler published in the programme for the 1978 production in Milan, translated by the present author.

Strongly influenced by the criticism of Kott, he examined the sense of futility in the play, taking up the Polish critic's assertion that the theatre cannot change life, and turning the enquiry into an analysis of artistic issues relevant to his own status as director:

> *The Tempest* is a desperate work. It is the most poignant lament over the failure of a marvellous humane project, a project which has not succeeded. As well as posing fundamental questions about life itself and history, about the knowledge that Shakespeare imparts to us in *The Tempest* there are questions about the purpose of theatrical effect. That is to say questions about how and why we – the people involved with the stage – create theatre, questions about what theatre should be and could be.

For Strehler, Shakespeare's last play shared some of the fascination of Pirandello's (unfinished) final work *The Mountain Giants*. He saw *The Tempest* as being fundamentally concerned, as are the dramas of the Italian playwright, with the ambiguous relationship of art to life. 'In this production, as never before,' he concluded, 'we have felt the fallible, desperate triumphant grandeur and responsibility of our profession.'

Strehler's production opened with a spectacular storm lasting fifteen minutes. Behind a huge transparent canvas an open-sailed ship was visible. Sailors clambered up the ropes; the rigging collapsed; the mast split. Throughout this scene vast blue waves billowed and rolled round the stage, created by huge lengths of blue silk – five thousand square yards of it – operated by sixteen unseen operators hidden under the stage, which was divided into three corridors with their floor shaped into mounds and hollows. Musicians beat drums, stage hands operated thunder sheets, and technicians provided bursts of lightning. It was in two senses a 'direful *spectacle*': terrifying but at the same time clearly the product of theatrical artifice. Finally the waves retreated as the strips of silk were drawn back to reveal a simple wooden raft which represented the island.

This opening scene set the note of the production which was to centre on Prospero and Ariel, converting their relationship into a metaphor for the interaction of director and actor. Ariel was played by Giulia Lazzarini as a sad white-faced pierrot suspended from a clearly visible theatrical cable. This prop, too, assumed metaphorical significance: when Prospero refused his servant's freedom, Ariel tugged at the cable in a desperate attempt to be free. It represented the actor's dependence on the director rather than the slave's subservience to the master. Ariel was willing to play any role demanded by the director. Prospero's question, 'Hast thou, spirit, / Performed to point the tempest that I bade thee', had a fresh emphasis on the word 'performed'. Ariel replied by executing a series of balletic movements high in the air, the cable swinging out from side to side, in an intensely physical as well as verbal response. Having been sent by Prospero to fetch Ferdinand, (he/she returned dressed as 'a nymph o' the sea', reeling Ferdinand in on a fishing rod from the depths of the orchestra pit).

The scene which assumed the greatest significance in the production was that of the vanishing banquet and Ariel's appearance as a harpy [III iii]. As the courtiers were about to approach the food, the stage darkened and a hideous apparition with a human head, the body of a bird and equipped with huge talons came screeching down from the flies. At the same time the blue silk waves returned to lap round the island and virtually once again to engulf the guilty men. Ariel's warning, a hoarse scream of defiance, produced the most intense response as Alonzo rushed off-stage and Antonio and Sebastian followed like maddened animals. Powerful physical emphasis was given to Gonzalo's description: 'Their great guilt / Like poison given to work a great time after / Now 'gins to bite the spirits.' In the previous scene of the assassination attempt on Alonzo, Strehler also gave added theatrical force to the charming of the court to sleep by having Ariel throw a handful of sand into each person's eyes in turn. The fact that Antonio and Sebastian were left out was not the careless mistake which some directors commit when, in having Ariel perform magical waves of the hand over everyone but Antonio and Sebastian, they give the impression that Prospero has intended the conspiracy to take place. In Strehler's conception the dangers of the wicked lords were deliberately minimised; Ariel watched them carefully, intent on returning to thwart their plan.

For the same reason the betrothal masque was omitted from Strehler's 1978 production. Instead, Ferdinand and Miranda were seen relaxing against an idyllic background of sea and sky which clouded over when the rebels approached. Again, a group of characters – Trinculo, Stephano and Caliban – were established as firmly within Prospero's power since Ariel had been seen to accompany their antics on a tabor and pipe. Strehler's most impressive achievement was to integrate the comic scenes in a powerfully original way. Instead of being variations on the political theme they became further extensions of the concern with theatrical issues central to the conception. They were played as masked clowns from the *commedia dell'arte*: Trinculo as a Neapolitan Pulcinella (Punch), Stephano as the sinister figure of Brighella (with a corresponding accent of the Bergamo district of Northern Italy) – and his interpreter would later take on the role of the bullying braggart Captain. The comic gags and extended set pieces of buffoonery – such as the discovery of the monster with four legs and two voices, or the interruptions of Ariel which lead to the beating of Trinculo – emphasised the drama's dependence on the Italian comic tradition. The repeated attempts in English productions (both the Brook and the Hall versions, for instance) to give life to these scenes by acting them in the manner of music hall, with Stephano played as a George Robey character, misinterpret the essential nature of Shakespeare's inspiration and are unable to match the theatrical versatility of true *commedia*.

In Strehler's production, when the court fled after the apparition of the harpy they left behind them their robes and Alonzo his crown. Ariel, now as stage manager, carefully collected them and placed them in a props cupboard under the stage. They were taken out of this and given to Trinculo and Stephano later when they were beguiled by the glittering wardrobe. Hence, the repeated image of the 'borrowed robes', which converts Stephano into a mini-Macbeth, was given a new twist. As doubles of their more dangerous corollaries, Antonio and Sebastian, they further enforced the mirror-image which is characteristic of both Shakespeare and Pirandello in their exploitation of the relationships between theatre and life.

Because no real threat was offered to Prospero it was clear that Strehler's interpretation of the renunciation of magic arts would be unconventional. Here Prospero did not abandon his art because he had become too wrapped up in it, but because he had exhausted its potential. The theatrical artist cannot commit himself too deeply; he must, however, realise when to stop. Ariel's prompting in this context took on a new meaning. It became the warning to the artist – specifically here to the director – that he was using his 'meaner ministers' (his actors) thoughtlessly. Ariel, subsequently released, crossed over the ramp covering the orchestra pit and disappeared through the audience. Yet Strehler had another, final *coup de théâtre* in store. Prospero's epilogue came firmly into its own as the theatrical artist's apology for the limitations of his magic. It had proved unable to transform everything; certain obdurate elements in the world will always remain impervious to its charms. As the play ended and the epilogue began, the wooden stage floor noisily split open and a heavy safety curtain crashed down, partially covering the proscenium. The audience's response to Prospero's plea for indulgence – their applause – caused the safety curtain to fly up, the stage to reassemble and Ariel to return and stand by his/her master. Kott, who was invited to Milan for the production and who was highly critical of it, commented: 'The surprising, disturbing, yet touching identification of the director with the character of the drama, of Strehler with Prospero, is the source of all the revelations and enchantments of the Milan *Tempest*, as well as all its limitations' ('Prospero or the Director', *Theatre* [Yale: Spring 1979]). There can be no doubt, however, that the many strokes of theatrical magic in this production served to enrich the meaning of a familiar play.

Kott's mistrust of the many spectacular stage effects in Strehler's production found an echo in the reaction of several English critics to the Peter Hall version of 1974. In his diaries Hall records the profound impression made on him by Roy Strong's and Stephen Orgel's two-volume study, *Inigo Jones: The Theatre of the Stuart Court*. 'After this book', he comments, 'one understands the masque – and that it is a very different form to the drama. It is a wonderful study for *The Tempest*' (*Diaries*, p. 57). In a review of this study Hall further clarifies what was to influence his conception of the play realised three months later. He begins by drawing attention to what he sees as a basic problem of English theatre-going:

The English suspect the visual delights of the theatre. For centuries the drama has been studied as literature. There is, therefore, an assumption that the play not only begins with the word, but had better end with it as well; otherwise it is inferior, appealing more to the eye than the ear. The puritan distrust of emblems, of representation by symbol and artifice, is a recurrent national neurosis. Out of this tension we have produced two of the supreme visionaries of the theatre: Edward Gordon Craig and Inigo Jones.

(*Sunday Times*, 16 December 1973)

'Jones's designs', Hall argues, 'demonstrate the shifting contradictions of life with the ease of poetry. And if they are done well and seriously, they can have the same effect today. Spectacle is the chief instrument of the masque, as music is of the opera. It excites wonder. Out of that wonder comes meaning.' This emphasis on the significance of visual images, stage metaphors as pointers to an understanding of the work, was basic to his realisation of *The Tempest*. It forms an interesting parallel with Strehler's approach; and in allerting us to the conflict of literary and theatrical values, brings our study to a fitting conclusion.

Hall made the masque the dominant structure of the play as a whole, with Prospero supervising in the role of stage manager. Though dressed to look like Doctor Dee, Gielgud more properly resembled Inigo Jones, the architect and purveyor of deeper meaning through his stage imagery. The artificiality of the set was underlined from the start. The sliding flats in the manner of Jones's later entertainments, such as *Salmacida Spolia* of 1640, effected scene-changes rapidly and economically. An orange sun suspended on two visible cords hung from the sky. The costumes were extravagant, notably for the spirits serving the banquet and the goddesses of the betrothal masque-within-a-masque, one of whom – Juno – was made to resemble the dead Queen Elizabeth: thus hinting at the lost Tudor world of Renaissance potential.

As with Strehler's production, it was the presentation of Ariel which was the most original and illuminating aspect of the staging. Michael Feast played him as an androgynous figure, descending from the flies on a thin bone-like structure. He was spirit, clinging desperately to the last remnants of the body: a powerful visual image summing up one of the most profound concepts of neo-platonic philosophy. Significantly, Prospero never looked at him. Gielgud has made a point in all four of the productions in which he has appeared of never confronting Ariel face to face. In the Hall staging this further emphasised the role of Ariel as a spiritual extension of his master. In this character Hall most forcefully realised the potential of visual theatrical metaphor to convey a precise and complex significance. A vivid and more meaningful stylisation had been found in Hall's Old Vic version than that which had served – and proved so influential – in previous productions at the same theatre. Leslie French's beautiful and lithe dancer of 1930 had inspired Eric Gill's statue outside Broadcasting House. Elsa Lanchester's ethereal creature of 1934 had strong affinities with the Bride of Frankenstein she was to play in James Whale's celebrated film the following year. These were visual references of a different order. Hall's approach served to illuminate the ethical concepts central to the play.

Hall was right to castigate the English distrust of the non-verbal in the theatre. His production was criticised as being an empty show, distracting the audience from the play's poetry. All of the four versions of the play we have examined in detail elicited a strong measure of critical hostility. This will always be the case in a theatrical tradition governed by literary criteria. England has produced too many dramatists – Shakespeare paramount among them – for the skill of the director ever to be taken as seriously as that of the writer: a situation which does not obtain in other parts of Europe. Yet a director of intellectual integrity and imagination can offer more valuable and effective insights than the literary critic. Moreover, his interpretation is put more firmly to the test on stage than that of the closeted commentator who need never trouble himself with considerations of the play in performance.

In assessing the respective contributions of the critic and director, it is salutary to end with the comments of a man of the theatre who has distinguished himself in both fields. This is the assertion of Charles Marowitz – an attitude worthy of serious and lengthy consideration by any student of Shakespeare:

> The question is not, as is so often put, what is wrong with Shakespeare that we have to meddle with his works, but what is

wrong with us that we are content to endure the diminishing returns of conventional dramatic reiteration: that we are prepared to go to the theatre and pretend that what dulls our minds and comforts our world-view is, by dint of such reassurances, culturally uplifting; not to realise that there is nothing so insidious as art that perpetuates the illusion that some kind of eternal truth is enshrined in a time-space continuum called 'a classic'; not to challenge the notion that its theatrical performance is *automatically* an experience because our assumption of a play's established worth guarantees us that experience. We all dupe ourselves in the theatre because we have been sold a bill of goods for a good quarter of a century before we enter. We get what we expect and we expect what we have been led to expect, and it is only when we don't get what we have been led to expect that we are on the threshold of having an experience.

(Introduction to *The Marowitz Shakespeare*, p. 25)

READING LIST

The student is advised to begin further enquiry by studying Frank Kermode's careful Introduction to the play in his New Arden edition of *The Tempest* (Methuen, London, 1954). This illustrates the strengths and weaknesses of literary criticism. It is a detailed exploration of the play's sources and themes but scarcely considers the work as drama, much less as theatre. Such an analysis is in key with the studies from Coleridge onwards which have tended to examine the play as essentially a dramatic poem. The most extreme expression of this tendency is Reuben A. Brower's essay in *The Fields of Light* (Oxford U.P., New York & London, 1951), which treats *The Tempest* as a 'Metaphysical poem of metamorphosis' in the manner of Marvell's *The Garden*. This critical tradition incorporates several celebrated studies:

J. Middleton Murry, *Shakespeare* (Cape, London, 1936): emphasising the beneficent effect of the sea-change on all the characters, and seeing the play as 'Shakespeare's dream';

E. M. W. Tillyard, *Shakespeare's Last Plays* (Chatto & Windus, London, 1938): stressing the theme of forgiveness and drawing attention to the play's lack of dramatic tension;

Wilson Knight, *The Crown of Life* (Methuen, London, 1947): treating the play as a summation of all Shakespeare's previous work, claiming that 'the people scarcely exist in their own right';

Frank Davidson, '*The Tempest*: An Interpretation', in *Journal of English and German Philosophy*, 62 (Illinois U.P., Urbana, 1963): a more penetrating study, drawing attention to the importance of the 'revenge' theme and Prospero's consequent difficulty in forgiving his enemies.

Key extracts from all the works listed in this section are conveniently reproduced in D. J. Palmer (ed.), *The Tempest*, in the Casebook series (Macmillan, London & Basingstoke, 1968), along with other material representing critical viewpoints from the late seventeenth century to the present day.

Of the above, only Davidson's article emphasises dramatic issues which have a bearing on staging. Palmer's selection – with one exception (see below re. Kott) – is exclusively of literary criticism. Nor does he include the important and challenging attack on the last plays by Lytton Strachey, in his essay 'Shakespeare's Final Period', first published in *Books and Characters* (Chatto & Windus, London, 1922).

PERFORMANCE ASPECTS

In addition to Frank Davidson's article cited above, the student should consult Jan Kott's essay, 'Prospero's Staff', in his provocative study *Shakespeare Our Contemporary* (Methuen, London, 1964; Norton, New York, 1964). An excerpt from this is reproduced in the Casebook cited above. Kott's essay is one of three which all treat *The Tempest* as theatre and take up Strachey's thesis, seeing the play as a work of disillusion. His other two studies – one discussing the tragic theme of repetition, the other the play's employment of masque and its affinities with Virgil's *Aeneid* – are to be found in *Arcadia Amara* (Il Formichiere, Milan, 1978). Unfortunately no English translation is available.

Jan Kott's lengthy criticism of Giorgio Strehler's Milan production (1978), itself influenced by his writings, is published in *Theatre* (Yale School of Drama Publications, New Haven, Conn.: Spring 1979). Kott's work is far more incisive than the study by David William, '*The Tempest* on the Stage', in J. R. Brown & B. Harris (eds), *Jacobean Theatre*, Stratford-upon-Avon Studies, I (Edward Arnold, London, 1960).

Further information on Gielgud's different interpretations of Prospero are to be found in his most recent autobiography *An Actor and His Time* (Sidgwick & Jackson, London, 1979), and in *The Ages of Gielgud*, edited by Ronald Harwood (Hodder & Stoughton, London, 1984). Derek Jarman's highly entertaining autobiography *Dancing Ledge* (Quartet Books, London, 1984) contains an informative chapter (pp. 182–206) on the making of the *Tempest* film.

THEMATIC ASPECTS

For a fuller discussion of magic, two of Frances A. Yates's books are highly recommended:
Theatre of the World (Routledge, London, 1969; Chicago U.P., 1969);
The Occult Philosophy in the Elizabethan Age (Routledge, London, 1979).
The first-named explores in detail the links between occult philosophy and the structure of the Elizabethan and Jacobean theatre.

For further material on Inigo Jones and the staging conventions influencing *The Tempest*, the definitive work is Stephen Orgel and Roy Strong, *Inigo Jones: The Theatre of the Stuart Court* (Sotheby/Parke Bernet, London & New York, 1973). The gist of this can also be found in the copiously illustrated catalogue edited by Orgel and Strong for the quatercentenary exhibition at the Banqueting House, Whitehall:

The King's Arcadia – Inigo Jones and the Stuart Court (Arts Council of Great Britain, London, 1973).

For fuller discussion of the nature and significance of Renaissance tragicomedy see the study by the present author: *Tragicomedy* in the Critical Idiom series (Methuen, London, 1984).

INDEX OF NAMES

FOR READER'S NOTES

FOR READER'S NOTES

FOR READER'S NOTES

FOR READER'S NOTES

FOR READER'S NOTES